Berklee

CONTEMPORARY

Dictionary *of*
MUSIC

DR. KARI JUUSELA

Berklee Press

Editor in Chief: Jonathan Feist
Vice President of Online Learning and Continuing Education: Debbie Cavalier
Assistant Vice President of Operations for Berklee Media: Robert F. Green
Assistant Vice President of Marketing and Recruitment for Berklee Media: Mike King
Dean of Continuing Education: Carin Nuernberg
Editorial Assistants: Emily Jones, Eloise Kelsey
Consulting Editor: Tatiana Holway
Cover Design: Small Mammoth Design

ISBN 978-0-87639-161-7

1140 Boylston Street
Boston, MA 02215-3693 USA
(617) 747-2146

Visit Berklee Press Online at
www.berkleepress.com

Study with

■ **BERKLEE ONLINE**

online.berklee.edu

DISTRIBUTED BY

HAL•LEONARD®
CORPORATION
7777 W. BLUEMOUND RD. P.O. BOX 13819
MILWAUKEE, WISCONSIN 53213

Visit Hal Leonard Online at
www.halleonard.com

Berklee Press, a publishing activity of Berklee College of Music, is a not-for-profit educational publisher.
Available proceeds from the sales of our products are contributed to the scholarship funds of the college.

CONTENTS

PREFACE

The world of contemporary music is constantly evolving. Any listener can hear the changes—some subtle, some startling. The ways we talk about music are changing, as well. New terms for describing the processes of writing, playing, and recording music circulate freely among performers, composers, arrangers, conductors, theorists, music technologists, students, and educators. My goal in writing this dictionary of contemporary music is to provide a guide to the language of the music of today.

Such a project, by its nature, can never be conclusive. As a classical theorist observed back in the early eighteenth century, the study of music is like an immense ocean, impossible for one person to navigate in a lifetime. True enough—and that was well before jazz, rock, hip-hop, country, contemporary classical, gospel, blues, Broadway, and film music were even thought of or heard. With a subject so vast, this dictionary cannot be a comprehensive index of all musical terms, but it does include over three thousand that contemporary musicians commonly use in their creative endeavors.

Reflecting the wide-ranging curriculum of the Berklee College of Music, this dictionary joins in the school's mission of teaching music through the music of our time. It has also benefited from the knowledge of Berklee musicians themselves, and I would like to thank my colleagues for their generosity in suggesting terms drawn from their areas of expertise and for their advice in honing definitions.

For my own part, researching and writing this dictionary has been wonderfully engaging. I hope readers will find it interesting and illuminating, as well as useful for their own musical journeys.

Abbreviations and Foreign Language Terminology

Instrument and vocal part names are abbreviated and capitalized to reflect the way that they appear in scores.

Translations of common score notations, while occasionally including literal meanings, are phrased in the way that they are typically used by English-speaking musicians.

Since the words we use to talk about music are so broadly multilingual, many non-English terms necessarily appear here, with translations as needed. The original language, however, is cited only with foreign-language score notations.

Non-American English terms are preceded by their language of origin, abbreviated as follows:

[Br.] British

[Fr.] French

[Ger.] German

[Heb.] Hebrew

[It.] Italian

[Lat.] Latin

[Port.] Portuguese

[Sp.] Spanish

Dictionary

1/8-inch jack. A phone connector (audio) of 1/8-inch diameter.

1/4-inch jack. A phone connector (audio) of 1/4-inch diameter. Often used for guitar-to-amplifier connections.

5.1. A six-channel surround system consisting of two front left/right speakers, two surround speakers, one center speaker, and one subwoofer.

8-bit music. See chiptune.

8-track. A magnetic audio tape and playback system with four pairs of stereo tracks.

12-string guitar. A guitar with twelve strings, in pairs tuned an octave apart.

12-tone serialism. See serialism.

12-tone technique. See serialism.

30-second spot. Radio or television advertising segment that is thirty seconds in duration.

45. A vinyl recording rotating at forty-five revolutions per minute. Often, with one song on each side.

60-second spot. Radio or television advertising segment that is sixty seconds in duration.

78. A vinyl recording rotating at seventy-eight revolutions per minute.

a [It.]. To, in, by, or at.

A. Abbr. for alto in vocal music.

a2. Played by two (both) instruments.

AAA. Abbr. for Adult Album Alternative, a radio format that features rock, pop, country, Americana, world music, blues, and folk music, but generally not rap, hip-hop, or heavier rock or metal. Also referred to as "triple-A."

AABA. A musical form that has a repeated section A that is followed by a contrasting section B and a return of the first section A.

AIFF. Abbr. for Audio Interchange File Format, an uncompressed professional-level audio file format.

ABA. A three-part musical form that has a repeated A section following the B section.

abandonné [Fr.]. Free, unconstrained.

abbandono [It.]. With abandon.

abbreviated pedal. (1) A short pedal point. (2) A sustained root or fifth in the bass occurring with other left-hand activity.

A. Bs. Abbr. for acoustic bass.

absolute music. Music composed with no extra-musical, nonrepresentational intent.

absolute pitch. See perfect pitch.

abstract music. See absolute music.

AC. Abbr. for Adult Contemporary radio format.

a cappella [It.]. (1) Sung without instrumental accompaniment, "as in the chapel." (2) A vocals-only track.

a capriccio [It.]. At the performer's pleasure.

accel. Abbr. for accelerando.

accelerando [It.]. Progressively increase the tempo.

accelerometer. An electrical device that senses motion.

accent. A stress or emphasis placed on a note or beat.

acciaccatura [It.]. In piano playing, to play and then release part of a chord.

accidental. A symbol preceding a note indicating a chromatic alteration of the pitch.

accompaniment. A musical backing of a soloist or a group. Also see comp.

accordion. A bellows-driven, arm-held, box-shaped, reeded wind instrument that is played using a keyboard and/or buttons. Also called a "squeezebox."

acid. See acid rock.

acid jazz. Jazz music coupled with elements of acid rock.

acid rock. A 1960s rock music style often featuring long open improvisations and psychedelic themes. The term comes from slang for LSD (lysergic acid diethylmide).

acousmatic. (1) Music and/or sound whose source remains unseen. (2) Electronic or computer music that is solely played through loudspeakers.

acoustical phase. A particular point in the cycle of a sound wave, measured as an angle in degrees.

acoustic bass. See contrabass.

acoustic guitar. A guitar with no built-in electronic amplification.

acoustic piano. A nonelectronic piano.

acoustics. (1) The study of mechanical waves in liquids, solids, and gasses. (2) The quality of the sound of a hall or space.

action. (1) The height of the strings above the fingerboard of a string instrument. (2) The mechanical assembly of a keyboard instrument. (3) The feeling of heaviness or lightness when depressing the keys of a keyboard instrument.

active electronics. Electronics in an instrument or device, which can control volume and other audio parameters.

active monitor. A loudspeaker that has electronics that can control audio parameters such as EQ, filtering, and loudness.

active pickup. A guitar, bass, or other instrument pickup that requires power in order to control audio parameters such as volume, EQ, etc.

adagietto [It.]. A bit faster than adagio.

adagio [It.]. Slowly.

ADAT. Alesis digital audio tape, a magnetic tape that records eight tracks of digital audio onto Super VHS tape.

ADC. Analog-to-digital converter.

added sixth. See sixth chord.

additive synthesis. A technique that creates complex waves by the addition of sine waves. See sound synthesis.

ad lib [Lat.]. Abbr. for ad libitum.

ad libitum [Lat.]. Improvised at the discretion of the performer.

ADSR. Attack, decay, sustain, release. See envelope.

a due [It.]. Played by two (both) instruments. See a2.

adult album alternative. A broad, diverse, alternative radio-play format, which is a contemporary version of the 1960s and 1970s rock-album format.

adult contemporary radio. A radio format which plays primarily easy listening, soft rock, soul, and light R&B music.

Aeolian harp. A variably sized and shaped instrument consisting of a frame with strings stretched across it, which vibrate and sound as air currents pass over them.

Aeolian mode. (1) A diatonic scale consisting of the notes A, B, C, D, E, F, G, A or one of its transpositions. (2) One of the eight modes used in Gregorian chant; later became known as the natural minor scale of the major/minor tonal system. See Scales in the Appendix.

aerophone. Instruments that create sound by causing a body of air to vibrate (e.g., trumpets, flutes, harmonicas, sirens).

AES. Audio Engineering Society.

affetuoso [It.]. Tenderly, warmly, affectionately.

affretando [It.]. Pushing ahead in tempo.

AFM. American Federation of Musicians.

afoxé. (1) A gourd-shaped, shaken rattle used in Afro-Brazilian music. (2) A traditional Afro-Brazilian music style.

African fingerstyle. A guitar technique originating in Africa in which the player uses just the thumb and one finger of the plucking hand.

African jazz. South African music style combining South African marabi with American swing.

Afrobeat. Musical style popularized in Nigeria in the 1970s featuring call and response, chanting, and complex polyrhythms. A mix of highlife, funk, jazz, and Yoruba music.

Afro-Cuban. A musical style that developed in Cuba from a combination of Spanish and African influences.

Afro-pop. A general term for any style of contemporary African popular music.

Afro-samba. African-influenced Brazilian musical style.

aftertouch. A technical enhancement on a pressure-sensitive keyboard, which gives the ability to affect parameters of the sound after a key has been depressed.

AFTRA. American Federation of Television and Radio Artists.

afuche. See cabasa.

agent. A person who represents the interests of a creative artist such as a musician or composer. See booking agent.

agitato [It.]. Agitated, restless.

agité [Fr.]. Agitated, restless.

agogic accent. Stress given to a note emphasized by extending its duration.

agogo. African-Brazilian percussion instrument made of iron or zinc with two bells played with a metal stick.

A. Guitar. Abbr. for acoustic guitar.

Ahavoh Rabboh scale. A Hebrew scale used often in klezmer music. See Scales in the Appendix.

alap. A slow, improvised, free-time introduction to a raga in Indian classical music.

al fine [It.]. (1) To the end. (2) A direction, as after dal segno or da capo, to play to the end.

al segno [It.]. (1) To the sign. (2) A direction to play to the sign.

aleatory. A musical style in which the element of chance is employed in the compositional process or in the performance.

Alexander technique. A technique originally developed by Shakespearean actor Frederick Alexander to alleviate tension in order to free the speaking and singing voice, but now used by many musicians and others in order to maintain physical and mental balance in their activities.

algorithm. A set of rules or procedures for solving a problem, now typically used in computer applications.

algorithmic music. Music created using step-by-step formulas, often with the aid of a computer.

aliasing. Digital distortion and fold-over that occurs when the sampled frequency is more than one-half the sample rate. See Nyquist frequency.

alla [It.]. In the style of.

alla breve [It.]. Following the half note as the beat unit. See cut time.

allargando [It.]. Becoming slower and broader.

all-combinatorial row. In twelve-tone serial composition, a row that is combinatorial with any of its derivations and their transpositions.

allegretto [It.]. Slower than allegro.

allegro assai [It.]. Very fast.

Alleluia [Heb.]. (1) Literally, Praise ye Jah. (2) A Christian liturgical chant in which the word "alleluia" is interspersed with verses of scripture.

almglocken. A set of oval-shaped Swiss cowbells.

alphorn. A long wooden horn of Swiss alpine origin.

alt. (1) A chord suffix indicating an altered chord. (2) See alternative rock.

altered chord. (1) In jazz harmony, a dominant 7 chord with tensions ♭9, ♯9, ♭5, and ♭13. (2) In classical harmony, another name for a chromatic harmony (e.g., a secondary dominant).

altered dominant scale. A scale often used to improvise over altered dominant chords. The scale is derived from a dominant 7, ♭9, ♯9, ♯11, and ♭13 chord (e.g., C, D♭, E♭, E, F♯, A♭, B♭).

altered scale. See altered dominant scale.

altered tension. Chromatically raised or lowered extended tensions (e.g., ♭9, ♯9, ♭13) on a chord.

altered tuning. See alternate tuning.

alternate fingering. An optional instrumental fingering provided by an editor or composer in a musical score or part.

alternate fingers. Instrumental technique of using a different finger on a repeated note.

alternate mix. A new mix of a recording in which the original elements have been changed.

alternate tuning. Deliberately tuning a stringed instrument to other than its standard tuning. See scordatura.

alternative. See alternative rock.

alternative rock. A genre of rock music originating in the 1980s with roots outside of the mainstream commercial radio-play music.

alto. (1) The lowest female vocal range in choral music, typically, G3 to D5. (2) Abbr. for *alto saxophone.

alto clef. A C clef with middle C indicated on the third line of a staff.

alto flute. A lower-sounding, transposing, transverse flute in the key of G, with a normal range of G3 to G6.

alto saxophone. An E♭ transposing, single-reed woodwind instrument of the saxophone family, with a normal range of D♭3 to A5.

AM. (1) Abbr. for amplitude modulation, a method for transmitting information using a carrier wave. (2) The earliest widely used method for radio broadcast.

am Frosch [Ger.]. At the frog (bowing technique).

AM radio. Radio using amplitude modulation for sound broadcast. Widely used and most important commercial radio transmission method until FM transmission began after World War II.

amabile [It.]. Amiable.

ambichord. A chord with a hybrid voicing, which has an ambiguous sound due to the omission of the third and emphasis of one or more harmonic tensions.

ambience. The tone quality or sound of a recording or space. Often used to refer to the amount of reverberation in a space or recording.

ambient drum and bass. A drum and bass subgenre influenced by New Age ambient music.

ambient music. Electronic and New Age music that often features a large amount of reverberation.

ambient trip-hop. A subgenre of hip-hop music that mixes trip-hop music with ambient music.

amoroso [It.]. Lovingly, tenderly.

amp. Abbr. for amplifier.

amp head. A power amplifier that is housed in a separate box from its speaker cabinet(s).

amplifier. (1) An electronic device that increases the strength of an electrical signal. (2) A unit that includes a power amplifier and loudspeaker(s) to increase the loudness of an electric guitar, bass, keyboard, or other musical instrument or microphone.

amplitude. (1) Loudness of an audio wave as defined by the strength of an electrical signal or a digital representation of the signal. (2) The breadth of a vertical harmonic structure.

amplitude modulation. A method for transmitting information using a carrier wave.

anacrusis. See upbeat.

analog synthesizer. Voltage-controlled synthesizer.

analog tape. Magnetic recording tape.

analog-to-digital converter. A device that changes a voltage into a digital number.

anapest. Two weak rhythmic stresses followed by a strong rhythmic stress.

ancora [It.]. Once again.

andante [It.]. Moderate, walking tempo.

andantino [It.]. Faster than andante.

anechoic. Having no echo.

Anfang [Ger.]. Beginning.

angklung. Japanese rattle.

animato [It.]. Animated.

animé [Fr.]. Animated.

ankrasmation. A symbolic notation language created for improvisation by composer and trumpeter Ishmael Wadada Leo Smith.

anschwellen [Ger.]. Increasing (in loudness).

answer. In a fugue, the transposed subject (theme) that follows the initial subject (theme). If the answer is "real," it is an exact transposed copy of the subject. If it is "tonal," the transposed subject has been altered.

antecedent/consequent. A two-phrase structure characterized by a question/answer quality, which often creates a musical period.

antecedent phrase. The first of two consecutive phrases that together may create a period.

anthem. (1) A symbolic song that represents a group of people or organization. (2) A musical portion of the Anglican Church service roughly corresponding to a motet.

anthem rock. See arena rock.

antigroove. Accenting beats 1 and 3, thus preventing forward motion and syncopation.

antiphon. (1) A hymn or a psalm that is chanted or sung in an alternating fashion by two groups of singers. (2) A section of the Catholic mass.

anvil. A solid metal block that is struck with a hammer or mallet.

aperto [It.]. Open.

a piacere [It.]. At the performer's pleasure, freely.

A. Pno. Abbr. for acoustic piano.

apoyando. A rest stroke in classical guitar playing in which the plucking finger comes to rest on the next string following a pluck.

appassionato [It.]. With passion.

appoggiatura [It.]. See leaning tone.

approach chord. A harmonized approach note, that in a soli texture, resolves to a target chord.

approach note. A general category of nonchord tone, either prepared (preceded by stepwise motion) or unprepared (preceded by leap), that resolves by step to a chord tone. Specific types of approach notes include passing tones and neighbor tones. In a concerted, soli texture, approach notes are often reharmonized.

a punta d'arco [It.]. At the tip of the bow.

A&R. Artists and Repertory. A person or record company department responsible for finding new talent and deciding which songs to record.

Arabesk. Turkish music with Arabic melodies and style.

Arabesque. A highly embellished, filigreed, and ornate classical composition whose style reflects the intricacies of Arabic architecture.

Arabic scale. See double harmonic minor scale.

archtop guitar. A steel-string, hollow-body acoustic or electric guitar that features violin-like f-holes and a convex top instead of the more typical flat top.

arco [It.]. Bowed (string instruments).

arduino. A single-board microcontroller often used in music to create voltage-controlled synthesizer components.

arena rock. Rock music that is written for, or to sound like, performance in large arenas.

aria. A piece for a solo singer, usually within a larger work like an opera.

armonico [It.]. Harmonic.

arpeggiator. A feature on electronic organs and synthesizers, primarily during the 1960s through the 1980s, that created arpeggios of chords predetermined or created by the performer.

arpeggio [It.]. A broken chord.

Arp Odyssey. An electronic synthesizer invented by American engineer Alan R. Pearlman in 1969.

arrangement. A reharmonization, reorchestration, and/or reformation of an existing melody or piece of music.

arrow. An analytical symbol showing dominant-to-tonic chord movement.

arrow sheet. A lead sheet with arrows that indicate the direction of the bass.

ars antiqua [Lat.]. Ancient art. A thirteenth-century Medieval musical style that flourished just prior to the ars nova.

ars nova [Lat.]. New art. A French and Burgundian musical style of the fourteenth-century Medieval period.

articulation. A performance technique that indicates or describes how individual notes and transitions between notes are sounded.

artificial harmonics. On a string instrument, overtones that are not part of the instrument's open-string harmonic series and are produced by a stopped string.

artist. See music artist.

artistic identity. Characteristics such as style and presentation that define a musician's persona.

artistic intention. Planned goals, impact, and direction of a musician's creations.

artistic vision. The essential conceptual frame for an artist's work.

art music. Contemporary music that is an outgrowth of the European classical music tradition. Usually, features advanced theoretical concepts and is in the written music tradition. Also referred to as "serious music," "legitimate music," "legit music," and "contemporary classical music."

art rock. A form of rock music from the 1960s that was influenced by classical, jazz, and experimental music. Later, it evolved into progressive rock (also referred to as "prog rock").

art song. A piece for voice and usually piano, written in the classical or contemporary classical tradition. Most often intended for concert or voice recital performance.

art techno. See intelligent dance music.

A. Sax. Abbr. for alto saxophone.

ASCAP. American Society of Composers, Authors, and Publishers, a performing rights organization.

assai [It.]. Very.

assez [Fr.]. Enough, fairly.

a tempo [It.]. Resume tempo.

atonal. Music that usually utilizes the chromatic scale and lacks a key center, central pitch, or tone.

A Train ending. The melodic figure that ends Billy Strayhorn's "Take the A Train," a signature song of the Duke Ellington Orchestra (C, E, F, F♯, G, A, B, C).

attacca [It.]. Suddenly, with no pause.

attenuator. An electronic device, or its digital equivalent, that reduces the strength of a signal.

audiation. See inner hearing.

audio. Generally, sound; more particularly, electrical or digital transmission and reproduction of sound.

audio engineer. A person who records, edits, and mixes sound and music for digital and analog recordings, films, television programs, video games, and other media.

Audio Interchange File Format. A 44.1 kHz uncompressed digital-audio file format. Often abbreviated AIFF or AIF.

audio interface. A connecting device, often with an analog-to-digital convertor (ADC) and a digital-to-analog convertor (DAC), that allows instruments and microphones to connect with a computer or DAW.

audio workstation. See DAW.

augmented. (1) An interval raised by a half step. (2) A major chord with a fifth raised by a half step. (3) A note value that is elongated.

aulos. A single- or double-piped reed wind instrument from the Classical period of ancient Greece.

au pointe d'archet [Fr.]. At the tip of the bow.

aural memory. Capacity for remembering what is heard.

aural training. The study and training of the ear to hear, notate, and sing intervals, chords, harmonies, timbres, and rhythms.

Auratone. Small reference speakers that gained the nickname "Horror Tone" due to their unembellished sound.

aussi [Fr.]. As, also.

authentic cadence. A harmonic cadence that ends V I.

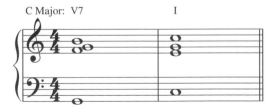

autoharp. A box-shaped stringed instrument played with buttons that trigger dampers to mute specific notes, thereby allowing the strings of intended chords to sound.

automation. In audio recording, a mechanical or digital system that allows aspects of a mixdown, such as level and panning, to occur in real time.

autonomous music. Music that does not involve strategy or games in its performance.

autosave. A function that is found in many computers and hardware devices that allows the user to save an active or open file automatically at specified intervals.

autotune. (1) A pitch correction and pitch manipulation plug-in. (2) The process of pitch correction, primarily for vocals.

aux. channel. Abbr. for auxiliary channel.

auxiliary channel. See auxiliary track.

auxiliary input. (1) An input through which audio signals can be passed (bussed) on an audio mixer. (2) A secondary audio input on a device such as an amplifier.

auxiliary percussion. Part of a band or orchestra percussion section that includes unpitched (untuned) percussion instruments such as the snare drum and triangle.

auxiliary send. A bus in a mixing console that sends an independent mix to an outside (auxiliary) device such as a reverb unit or effects processor.

auxiliary track. In a digital audio workstation (DAW), a destination track through which audio signals can be passed.

aux. input. Abbr. for auxiliary input.

aux. perc. Abbr. for auxiliary percussion.

aux. send. Abbr. for auxiliary send.

aux. track. Abbr. for auxiliary track.

available tension. In jazz-based harmony, a potential extended tertian (9, 11, 13) chord tone that is derived from the tonic key and does not obscure the harmonic function of the chord or create an unacceptable dissonance.

avec [Fr.]. With.

avoid note. In jazz-based harmony, melody, and improvisation, a scale degree that obscures the harmonic function of a chord and/or creates a strong dissonance.

ax. See axe.

axe. Name for a guitar or sometimes any instrument.

axé. Brazilian music style.

axis system. A system of harmonic substitution built around a chromatic circle of pitches with the minor thirds dividing the circle into quadrants.

ayre. A solo song, usually accompanied by lute, popularized in England during the late Renaissance.

B. Abbr. for bass in vocal music.

B-3. Abbr. for Hammond B-3 organ.

baby grand. A small (five- to six-foot case) grand piano.

baby scratch. A DJ turntable app with a built-in sampler.

back-door cadence. A IVmi7 ♭VII7 I harmonic cadence.

back-door progression. See back-door cadence.

backbeat. Heavy emphasis of beats 2 and 4 in 4/4 time.

backcycling. Harmonic root motion by descending fourths rather than by the stronger and more traditional descending fifths.

back end. Royalties acquired or payments made after a musical project has been completed.

background. The harmonic accompaniment supporting a melody line or lead vocal.

background vocalist. A singer who supports a primary singer by providing vocal harmonies and/or other backing vocals.

backstab. In turntable technique, a short, powerful burst of sound played backwards.

backup singers. Vocalists who accompany a lead singer.

baffle. (1) A partition, often used in speaker cabinets, to keep sound waves from interfering or canceling each other. (2) Materials and objects designed to reduce the loudness level or absorb sound energy to reduce reverberation.

bagatelle. A short classical composition, often for piano, in a light style.

bagpipes. An aerophone instrument with which sound is created by forcing air from a bag to vibrate enclosed reeds.

baião. (1) Northeastern Brazilian music style. (2) A section played by acoustic guitars in Brazilian canto do desafio style.

balalaika. Russian triangular three-stringed instrument.

balance. (1) The relative loudness between instruments in a live setting or in a mix. (2) To create a balanced signal.

Balinese Pelog scale. See Scales in the Appendix.

ballad. (1) A piece in a slow tempo. (2) A Medieval dance tune. (3) A narrative song.

banana connector. See banana plug.

banana plug. A single-wire electric male connector often used to connect components of stereo hi-fi systems.

band. (1) A musical ensemble. (2) A track on a recorded tape. (3) See concert band.

bandolón. A large mandolin.

band-pass filter. An analog or digital device that allows only the frequencies in a defined range to pass through while attenuating or rejecting those outside of the specified range. See comb filter.

banjo. A four-, five-, or six-stringed instrument of African origin that features a circular frame covered with a resonating material such as animal skin or plastic.

bank. See sound bank.

bansuri. Indian transverse wooden flute.

bar. A unit of time defined by the music's meter and shown in music notation by a vertical line at its start and its end. Also called a "measure."

Bar. Abbr. for baritone in vocal music.

bar chimes. A percussion instrument that has numerous small metal cylinders of indefinite pitch arranged from short to long, hung from a wooden bar, and played with the fingers or a stick. Also known as a "mark tree" or "chime tree."

bar form. A form used by the German Medieval Meistersingers and Minnesingers that consists of two stanzas of a similar melody followed by a contrasting stanza, thus creating an AAB form.

baritone. Male voice type between bass and tenor with a typical range of F2 to F4.

baritone horn. A low-sounding piston-valved brass instrument with a range from E2 to F5.

baritone saxophone. A low-sounding member of the saxophone family transposing down an octave and a major sixth, in the key of E♭, and with a range of C2 to A4.

baritone ukulele. The four-stringed instrument that is the second lowest member of the ukulele family and is usually tuned D3 G3 B3 E4.

barline. A vertical line that delineates one bar from the next.

Beginning Repeat   Regular Barline   Double Barline   Broken Barline   End Repeat   Final Barline

Baroque. A European classical music period between 1650 and 1725.

barre chord. A chord on a fretted string instrument where the first finger is held flat against multiple strings creating a temporary nut.

barrelhouse. A style of improvised piano jazz with its roots in two-beat boogie-woogie.

Bar. Sax. Abbr. for baritone saxophone.

Bartók pizzicato. On a stringed instrument, a pizzicato technique, attributed to Hungarian composer Bela Bartók, where the string is plucked forcefully and allowed to slap against the fingerboard creating a percussive attack. Also called a "snap pizz."

bar zero. An empty bar added at the beginning of a film score to allow a count-in or an edit.

Basie ending. See Basie tag.

Basie tag. A swing-jazz ending popularized by the Count Basie Orchestra that features a ♯IIdim7 passing diminished chord between the IImi7 and inverted I6 chord.

bass. (1) The lowest of the male vocal ranges with a typical range of E2 to C4. (2) Short for a bass guitar or acoustic bass. (3) The lowest part in a piece of music.

bass and drums. See drum and bass.

bass bar. In instruments of the violin family and some acoustic guitars, a wooden bar that acts as a brace and runs from the base of the neck to the bridge.

bass clarinet. A low-sounding member of the clarinet family that is pitched in B♭ and has a range of B♭1 to B♭5.

bass clef. A clef used by basses, cellos, bassoons, and many other low-range instruments to indicate pitch. Its F-clef symbol includes two dots surrounding the fourth line of a 5-line staff indicating that line is F (F3).

bass drop. A point in an EDM piece when the excitement is ratcheted up by adding a loud and low bass part to the mix.

bass drum. A large drum that produces a low tone of indefinite or definite pitch. When in a drum kit, it is sometimes referred to as the "kick drum" due to its use of a foot beater.

basset horn. A wooden, single-reed wind instrument and member of the clarinet family. Larger than the clarinet, it is distinguished by a curve or a bend in the middle and is most often in the key of F.

bass flute. A bass member of the flute family pitched one octave below the concert flute.

basso continuo [It.]. A method of musical accompaniment from the Baroque period in which a notated continuous bass line is played by the left hand of a keyboard instrument and is often doubled by a cello or bassoon, much in the manner of a jazz walking bass. Harmonies are indicated by figures written under the bass notes, and the resulting chords are left to be realized (improvised) by the keyboard player.

bassoon. A low-sounding double-reed woodwind instrument of the oboe family with a range of B♭1 to B♭4.

bass trap. An absorptive device designed to reduce low frequencies in a recording, performing, or listening space.

bass trombone. A low-sounding member of the trombone family with a range of C2 to G4.

bata drum. A wooden-shelled, hourglass-shaped, two-headed drum that is played with the hands.

bateria. (1) The percussion line or rhythm section in a Brazilian samba school. (2) Drum kit.

baton. A short stick used by a conductor to direct a musical ensemble.

battery. In a drumline, the section that marches out onto the field. Usually consisting of snare drums, bass drums, tenor drums, and cymbals.

battuta [It.]. Beat.

Bauhaus. An early twentieth-century German interdiciplinary school of music, visual arts, and architecture.

B-boy. A male hip-hop street dancer.

B-boying. A hip-hop dance tradition that is related to break dancing.

B. Cl. Abbr. for bass clarinet.

B. Dr. Abbr. for bass drum.

beam. A line that connects two or more consecutive eighth notes. Multiple beams connect notes of shorter duration.

beast. A performer of exceptional ability.

beat. (1) A unit of the primary pulse. (2) The underlying rhythmic pattern of a song.

beatboxing. Simulating beats, drums, percussion, and other instruments using the voice, tongue, lips, cheeks, and mouth, often in conjunction with a microphone.

Beat Detective. A tool for beat-mapping in Pro Tools.

beater. (1) A mallet used to play a percussion instrument. (2) The mallet in a kick drum pedal.

Beatle bass. A violin-shaped Hofner 500/1 electric bass popularized by the Beatles bassist Paul McCartney.

beat-making. The process of creating a rhythmically based track that is often used as the underpinning of a song.

beat-mapping. Using a tool in a digital audio application to determine the beats, pulses, and meter of a segment of recorded audio.

beat-matching. A DJ technique that creates a seamless transition from one record to another by making sure the tempos are the same or by manipulating the tempos in order to align the music on the two records.

beat-mixing. A DJ technique of simultaneously playing two songs that have the same or a complementary beat.

beats. Songs in pop music and hip-hop.

bebop. A jazz style developed in the 1940s that features fast tempos, often complex chromatic melodies and harmonies, and extended virtuosic improvisation.

bebop blues. In jazz, a twelve-bar blues progression enhanced with chord substitutions and secondary dominants.

behind the beat. (1) To play slightly after the ictus of a beat, thereby creating a laid-back feel. (2) To play late and out of tempo. Often referred to simply as "behind." See also drag.

bel canto [It.]. (1) Literally, beautiful singing. (2) An Italian vocal style that emphasizes a light tone, a seamless legato, agile technique, and graceful phrasing.

belting. A highly emotional vocal style characterized by loud singing that borders on shouting.

ben [It.]. Well.

bend. A sounded note followed by an upward or downward glissando.

berceuse [Fr.]. Lullaby that is typically simple and in 6/8 time.

B-girl. A female hip-hop street dancer.

Bg. Vox. Abbr. for background vocalist(s).

bichord. (1) A harmonic sonority (chord) formed by stacking one triad on top of another. For example: C E G + F♯ A♯ C♯. (2) An instrument with two strings.

bien [Fr.]. Well.

big band. A jazz ensemble with a standard instrumentation consisting of four trumpets, five saxes (two alto, two tenor, one baritone), four trombones (three tenor, one bass), drums, bass, piano, and guitar.

Billboard. A music magazine that publishes weekly sales, digital downloads, airplay, and streaming charts of top songs in a variety of genres. The Billboard Hot 100 is one of the most important *Billboard* charts.

binary form. A two-part form in which the parts are often related and repeated (AABB).

binary meter. A time signature that is divisible by two (e.g., 2/4, 4/4).

binaural. A recording that has been produced by placing recording microphones in a position mimicking a listener's ears.

biniou. Breton fiddle.

biomusic. Compositions utilizing sounds generated by animals and plants.

bird's eye. See fermata.

bis [It.]. (1) Twice. (2) To be repeated.

bit-crushing. A digital signal-processing technique through which the number of bits of a sample is reduced, thus creating a distorted version of the sample.

bit depth. In digital audio pulse-code modulation, the number of bits per sample. The higher the bit depth, the higher in resolution the sample.

bitonal. Using two different keys at the same time.

biwa. A Japanese plucked string instrument with four or five strings.

black metal. A subgenre of heavy metal music that features fast tempos, screamed vocals, lo-fi sounds, and often anti-Christian lyrics.

black out. A direction for the lights to be turned off, indicating that a show or concert is ready to begin.

black sound. Denotes the absence of frequencies, thus creating silence, as opposed to white noise that includes all frequencies.

bleed. (1) Unintended sound captured by a microphone when recording. (2) Sound recorded on one track of an analog tape that overlaps onto an adjacent track.

block chord. A chord or voicing wherein all the notes are sounded simultaneously. Often built under the melody notes and in rhythmic unison with the melody.

blow. To improvise over chord changes.

Blue Beat music. British name for ska and reggae originating from the eponymous 1960s record company.

blue-eyed soul. Soul and rhythm and blues music performed by white artists.

bluegrass. An American roots music form related to country music and infused with influences from the United Kingdom and Ireland.

blue note. An expressive note in jazz and blues that is played a half step or less under its major-scale counterpart. Most often ♭3, ♭5, and ♭7.

Blue Note. (1) A famous jazz club in New York City. (2) A record company founded in 1939 and specializing in recording great jazz artists.

blues ballad. A song in a slow-blues form that often emphasizes a character rather than a narrative.

blues harp. A harmonica used in blues, folk, and rock music.

blues major pentatonic scale. An altered major pentatonic scale that has both a major and minor third (1, 2, ♭3, 3, 5, 6).

blues scale. A major scale with the addition of ♭3, ♭5, ♭7 and its subsets (1, 2, ♭3, 3, 4, ♭5, 5, 6, ♭7, 7). See Scales in the Appendix.

BMI. Broadcast Music, Inc., a music rights organization.

BNC. Bayonet Neill–Concelman, an RF (radio frequency) connector often used with coaxial cable to transmit analog and serial digital interface video signals.

B.O. Abbr. for black out.

board tape. Temporary removable tape that is placed on a mixing console to label the channels.

bodhrán. Large Irish frame drum.

Boehm system. A keywork system for flutes invented by nineteenth-century inventor and flautist Theobald Boehm.

bois [Fr.]. Wood, woodwind.

bolero. A slow-tempo Latin musical form in 3/4 time.

bombard. Breton bagpipes.

bonang. Knobbed Indonesian gongs.

bone. Short for trombone.

bones. A hand-held, clapper-like percussion instrument made from two bones or two pieces of resonant wood.

bongo drums. A pair of connected wooden drums, small and larger, of Afro-Cuban origin.

bongos. See bongo drums.

boogie. A repetitive swing eighth, shuffle groove pattern.

boogie-woogie. African American blues-based music that features a repeating eighth-note bass pattern that drives the groove.

booking agent. A person who represents a musician, band, ensemble, or orchestra in securing performance opportunities.

boom stand. A microphone stand that has an arm that can be moved horizontally or at a desired angle.

bop. See bebop.

bossa nova [Port.]. A Brazilian music style that blends samba and jazz.

bottleneck. The top section of a glass bottle, cut off, and used to play slide guitar.

bouché [Fr.]. Literally, stopped with the hand. Used as a direction in horn playing.

bounce. In audio recording, moving and consolidating two or more tracks or a mix, to another single or stereo track.

bounce music. A style of New Orleans hip-hop.

bourdon. (1) A low stop on a pipe organ. (2) The drone pipe of a bagpipe. (3) The bass (lowest) string of a violin or other string instrument. (4) Bass.

bourrée [Fr.]. A musical style in a quick double-time from the French dance of the same name.

bouts. The upper and lower curved sides in instruments of the violin family.

bouzouki. A Greek string instrument with three or four courses of strings that are played with a pick.

bow. A wooden or synthetic stick with horsehair or a synthetic substitute attached to it and used to excite and vibrate the strings of a stringed instrument.

bowed psaltery. A modern version of a psaltery (or zither) that has been adapted to allow the strings to be bowed as well as plucked.

bowing. Performance markings on a score or part that indicate how a player is to use the bow, the most essential being the direction of the stroke (up or down).

box. (1) Accordion. (2) Computer, as in "inside the box."

bpm. Abbr. for beats per minute.

brace. A curved vertical score marking joining multiple staves to indicate that the staves are for a single instrument such as a piano or organ. Also to indicate a temporary division of an instrument section.

bracket. (1) An analytical symbol to show a relationship between two chords, with II V typically acting as a unit. (2) A straight vertical line that joins two or more staves that indicate a grouping of like instruments.

brain-wave composition. Music created by use of currents from electrodes attached to a composer's or performer's head.

brake drum. A metal percussion instrument made from the brake drum of a car.

brass. (1) The instrument section of a band, orchestra, or ensemble that is made up of cornets, trumpets, horns, trombones, euphoniums, and tubas. (2) Instruments from the brass family.

brass band. An ensemble that is made up of instruments from the brass family. It is often supplemented by percussion.

bravura [It.]. Boldly, with spirit.

break. (1) The divide between the chalumeau register and clarion register of a clarinet. (2) The divide between the lower and higher vocal registers. (3) A solo section in a song where an instrument or instrumental section is featured.

breakbeat. A subgenre of EDM that features syncopated rhythms and polyrhythms.

break dancing. An acrobatic form of street dancing that features head spins, body spins, flips, and other gymnastic-like movements. Often danced to hip-hop, soul, funk, and other highly rhythmic music.

breaker. A person who break dances.

breaking. See break dancing.

breath controller. A MIDI continuous input device that allows the player to control sound parameters with his or her breath.

breathing. See pumping.

breath mark. In a musical score or part, a symbol that indicates when a wind or brass player or vocalist should inhale. The symbol is also used to indicate when non-wind instruments should take a slight pause.

breve [Br.]. A double whole note. (A semibreve is one whole note.)

brevity work. An experimental composition of a very short length (often less than a few seconds).

bridge. (1) A frame that holds the strings off the body of a string instrument. (2) A contrasting section of a song that often links a verse and a chorus.

bridge block. The section of an acoustic guitar bridge that has holes through which the strings are passed and held in place by bridge pins.

bridge piece. A part of a guitar bridge that supports one or two strings and can be used to adjust the strings' height and length.

bridge pin. The wooden, plastic, or metal pins that hold down the guitar string at the bridge.

brillante [It.]. Sparkling, brilliant.

brio [It.]. Vigor.

British invasion. A term used to describe the huge influx of bands, like the Beatles and the Rolling Stones and their records, from Britain to the United States in the 1960s.

Brit-rock. British rock music that began with the British invasion.

broadside ballad. Sixteenth- and seventeenth-century British narrative songs printed on poor quality paper (broadsheet).

Broadway. (1) The street in New York City that is known for musical theater. (2) A style of music that has its roots in musical theater.

broken time. A groove with a steady beat but interspersed with improvised rhythms.

brushes. A pair of percussion beaters with bristles connected to a handle.

Bsn. Abbr. for bassoon.

B. Tbn. Abbr. for bass trombone.

bubblegum. A style of light, bright, upbeat pop music from the 1960s and 1970s, intended primarily for teenage audiences.

Buchla. A voltage-controlled synthesizer from the 1970s.

bucket mute. A mute for brass instruments that attaches to the rim of the bell, attenuates high frequencies, and produces a soft muffled tone.

buckwheat. See shape note.

buffer. A temporary data holding area in a computer used to process information.

bugle. A trumpet-like brass instrument without valves or pitch-altering mechanisms.

bull's-eye. See fermata.

Buma/Stemra. Rights society representing the interests of music authors in the Netherlands.

bumper. In broadcasting, a musical signature or theme usually fifteen seconds in length.

burn. To record or copy a compact disc.

bus. (1) To move audio signals from one channel or device to another. (2) An audio channel that relays signals.

bush ballad. An Australian narrative song popularized by early British settlers.

bus-powered. Describes a type of device that receives its power from a computer's USB port or powered USB hub.

butt-end splice. Variant of butt splice.

button. A final short ending chord at the end of a jazz composition or arrangement.

butt splice. (1) In either analog or digital audio and video editing, to join two pieces of tape with no overlap or transition. (2) The junction thus created.

buzz track. In film, an audio track with low-level ambient sounds used as a temporary track to cover awkward and unnatural silence until dialog and music are included.

buzz-wah mute. A cup mute for brass instruments with vibrating membranes that create a buzzing sound.

Byzantine scale. See double harmonic minor scale.

cabasa. A percussion shaker of African origin that was originally made from a seed-filled gourd. Now often constructed using steel chain wrapped around a cylinder.

caccia [It.]. (1) Hunt or chase. (2) A fourteenth-century form featuring two canonic upper parts and a noncanonic lower part.

cachucha. A Spanish solo dance form of Cuban origin in 3/4 or 3/8 meter.

cacophony. A group of harsh, dissonant sounds.

cadence. A close or ending of a harmonic or melodic segment that suggests either pause or finality. See also half cadence, deceptive cadence, plagal cadence, authentic cadence, full dominant cadence, feminine cadence, full jazz cadence.

cadence chord. In modal and nondiatonic harmony, a chord that is analogous to a traditional chord found in a cadential pattern; e.g., ♭IIMa7 to Imi completing a phrase in the Phrygian mode.

cadenza [It.]. An improvised solo within a larger work, such as a concerto; usually virtuosic and showy.

caesura. A musical symbol indicating a pause or a break.

caisse [Fr.]. Drum.

Cajun music. An upbeat music style from Louisiana heavily influenced by French Canadian settlers and featuring accordion, fiddle, and voice.

calando [It.]. More slowly and softly.

call-and-response. The alternation of leader and follower(s), typically, with solo voice followed by chorus or a group of instruments.

calliope. An instrument that makes sound when steam is forced through large pitched whistles. It can be played with a keyboard or automated like a music box.

calore [It.]. Warmth.

calypso. A highly rhythmic Afro-Caribbean style of music originating in Trinidad and Tobago and often sung in French Creole.

cambiata. A three-note melodic ornamentation in which the target tone is approached from a step below and a step above.

campagne in aria [It.]. To hold horn bells high.

cancan. An energetic and provocative French dance in 2/4 time featuring a chorus line performing high leg kicks.

cancellation. See phase cancellation.

canción [Sp.]. Song.

candomblé. Afro-Brazilian ritual religious music style.

cannon plug. See XLR connector.

canon. (1) A form of counterpoint in which a melody is strictly imitated by one or more parts. (2) The most important compositions in a specific musical style.

cans. Headphones.

cantabile [It.]. In a singing style.

cantata. An extended religious composition for voices and instruments featuring arias, recitatives, and choruses.

cantor. The principal singer in a cathedral, church, or synagogue.

cantus firmus [Lat.]. (1)Literally, fixed song. (2) The foundational fixed or given melody in a polyphonic composition or contrapuntal work.

canzonetta [It.]. A short song.

capo [It.]. (1) Head, top. (2) Abbr. for capotasto.

capotasto [It.]. A device that is attached across the fingerboard of a string instrument to shorten the strings and raise the pitch.

capstan. A rotating pin that moves tape over the recording and playback heads of an analog tape recorder.

capture. To record sound or video.

cardioid microphone. A unidirectional microphone with a heart-shaped pattern of sound sensitivity.

carillon. An instrument typically found in a bell tower, with a set of twenty-three bells that are played by using a keyboard or other mechanism.

Carnatic music. South Indian classical music.

carol. A joyful song often with a religious theme.

cartage. The cost of moving instruments, equipment, or other items from one place to another.

cascade effect. In arranging, an effect created by sequentially adding notes (usually of an extended chord).

cassa [It.]. Drum.

cassette. Short for compact cassette or musicassette, a small cartridge-style magnetic tape format for recording and playing music.

castanets. A percussion instrument constructed from a small pair of hollowed-out clamshell-shaped wooden discs joined together by string and held and played with one hand.

castrato. A male singer who has been castrated prior to reaching puberty in order to retain a soprano range voice.

cat. A cool, hip jazz or improvising musician. See also hepcat.

catch. (1) A round of two or more parts in which some words in the different parts come together to create a phrase that is often humorous in nature. (2) See Scotch snap.

Cb. (1) In percussion score instrumentation, abbr. for cowbell. (2) Abbr. for contrabass.

CC. (1) Abbr. for continuous controller. (2) Abbr. for creative commons.

C clef. A notational symbol (clef) placed at the beginning of a staff where the clef's center point indicates which line is middle C (C4).

CD, CD-R, CD-RW. Compact disc, recordable compact disc, rewritable compact disc.

CD-ROM. Compact disc read-only memory, a multimedia recording format that can be read but not written over.

cédez [Fr.]. A little slower.

Cel. Abbr. for celesta.

CELAS. Rights society representing EMI Publishing for pan-European licenses.

celesta. A keyboard instrument in which depressed keys trigger hammers to strike metal bars.

cello. The baritone member of the violin family, supported by an end pin, held between the knees, and played by bowing or plucking. Tuned C2, G2, D3, A3. (2) A shortening of "violoncello."

cellular composition. A method of composition using pitch-class sets and/or rhythmic sets.

cembalo. See harpsichord.

cent. A measure of pitch. One cent is 1/100 of a tempered semitone.

center frequency. In or on an equalizer, the frequency that is the exact one to which a given filter is tuned.

Ch. Abbr. for chimes.

cha-cha. A dance of Cuban origin that originally began on the second beat in common time and featured two eighth notes on beat 4, as in 2, 3, 4-and, 1. Now, it is often heard as 1, 2, 3-and, 4.

cha-cha ending. The ending gesture of a piece of music that uses the typical cha-cha-cha rhythm of two eighth notes followed by a short quarter note.

Cha - Cha - Cha

chaconne. A musical composition of Baroque origin that uses a repeating harmonic progression as the basis of melodic variations.

chaleur [Fr.]. Warmth.

chalumeau. A single-reed woodwind folk instrument that is the predecessor of the modern clarinet.

chalumeau register. The lowest register of the clarinet named after its predecessor, the chalumeau.

chamber group. A small ensemble of instruments, often one per part, dedicated to performing art music. Originally intended for performance in a small room (chamber) as opposed to a larger hall or auditorium.

chamber music. Music performed by a small ensemble of instruments, often one per part.

chart 35

chance music. Music that employs some kind of aleatoric process in its creation or performance.

changes. The chords of a song or piece of music, usually indicated by chord symbols on a lead sheet or score.

changing tones. See cambiata.

channel. An audio or MIDI pathway.

channel separation. The amount of bleed from one audio channel to another.

channel strip. A stand-alone device or discrete section of a mixing board or console that processes the output of an audio device. It usually has equalization, phantom power, and a preamp.

chanson [Fr.]. (1) Song. (2) A polyphonic and usually secular French song of the late-Medieval and Renaissance periods.

chant. (1) To sing words set to music in a repetitive rhythmic fashion, often on a single tone or simple melody. (2) Religious text of the early Catholic Church that is set to reciting tones and simple modal melodies.

chanty. See sea chanty.

chaos. A field of study in mathematics whose algorithms can be used in creating music. Used especially in computer-assisted composition.

Chapman stick. A guitar-like ten- or twelve-stringed electric instrument, whose strings are depressed with the fingers of both hands in order to facilitate playing more than one musical line simultaneously.

character notation. See shape note.

charanga. Cuban popular music from the 1940s that is heavily influenced by son.

charango. A small, lute-like, Andean ten-coursed stringed instrument traditionally made from the shell of an armadillo.

chart. (1) The notated arrangement of a piece of music. (2) A music industry list of top-selling songs.

chase. (1) The continuous synchronization between two analog audio/video devices. (2) The initial synchronization of a digital "slave" device to a master device.

chest tone. In vocal music, the lowest register of the voice thought to have been produced by chest resonance.

chest voice. Forceful singing in the lowest register with the breath pressed forcefully from the chest.

chevalet [Fr.]. The bridge of a string instrument.

Chicago blues. An urban musical style, originating in Chicago, that is a mix of swing jazz and Delta blues.

Chicago house. House-style EDM music produced in Chicago in the 1980s.

chickin' pickin'. A guitar picking style of popping the strings against the neck to create a percussive sound. Most often associated with country music.

chime bar. See bar chimes.

chimes. (1) A set of large bells, also known as a carillon. (2) A set of tubular bells (metal tubes) that hang vertically, are laid out like a keyboard pitched C4 to F5, and are played with rawhide or plastic hammers.

Chinese blocks. See muyu.

Chinese scale. See Scales in the Appendix.

chin rest. A slightly concave plastic or wooden attachment on a violin or viola on which the player's chin is placed while playing.

chip music. See chiptune.

chiptune. Electronic music made using the sound chips of old or discarded computers, videos games, and arcade games.

chitarra Italiana. A four- or five-stringed lute-shaped instrument popular in Italy during the Renaissance.

chitarrone. A bass version of the chitarra Italiana.

chiuse [It.]. Brassy.

chiuso [It.]. Stopped.

chocallo. A Latin American canister shaker that is filled with beads, seeds, rice, or sand.

choke. To suddenly mute a cymbal with the hand.

chopping. A string performance technique in which the bow is brought down on the strings at an angle and immediately stopped, thereby creating a crunching sound.

chops. (1) A player's technical ability on an instrument. (2) A reference to a performer's hands or lips.

chorale. (1) A hymn tune sung in the Lutheran Church. (2) A harmonization (usually in four parts) of a hymn tune. (3) A vocal group or choir.

chord. A set of three or more notes that are sounded simultaneously or arpeggiated. Chords are typically used to harmonize or accompany a melody.

chord frame. A visual grid of the neck and frets of a string instrument with dots showing where to place the fingers in order to sound specific chords.

chordophone. A musical instrument that creates sound through the vibration of strings stretched between two points.

chord scale. A set of stepwise pitches related to a chord symbol that provide a supply of notes compatible with the chord's sound and its tonal or modal function.

chord symbol. A marking on a lead sheet or score showing the letter name of a chord, its quality, and any notes to be played in addition to the basic triad.

chord tremolo. The rapid alternation of two segments of a chord to create a trembling effect.

choro. A Brazilian style of popular music that often features bossa nova and samba rhythms.

chorus. (1) A repeated section of a song, usually following a verse or prechorus, in which the words and melody are similar at each occurrence. (2) One complete time through the form of a tune. (3) A group of singers. (4) A signal-processed effect that replicates the sound of multiple similar sounds. (5) The refrain section of a song. See also refrain.

Christian rock. Rock music with Christian-themed lyrics.

chromatic. (1) A note that is not a member of a given major or minor scale. (2) Music that uses all of the twelve pitches.

chromatically enhanced. A melodic figure or single note that is embellished with half steps.

chromatic approach. A note or chord that moves to a target note from either a half step above or below.

chromatic harmonica. A harmonica that has a slide button that enables the performer to play all twelve tones of the chromatic scale.

chromatic scale. A set of all twelve pitches in an octave.

chuck. A guitar picking or strumming technique, primarily used in funk music, in which notes are dampened immediately after playing.

chunk. In certain DAWs, a section of either audio or MIDI digital information.

church mode. One of the eight scales used in early Christian religious music. They are: Dorian, Hypo-Dorian, Phrygian, Hypo-Phrygian, Lydian, Hypo-Lydian, Mixolydian, Hypo-Mixolydian, Aeolian, Hypo-Aeolian. See Scales in the Appendix.

cimbalom. A chromatic Hungarian hammer dulcimer with dampers.

cinematics. The process and art of making motion pictures.

circle of fifths. A circular diagram of the twelve major keys, their relative minor keys, and their corresponding key signatures. See also cycle 5.

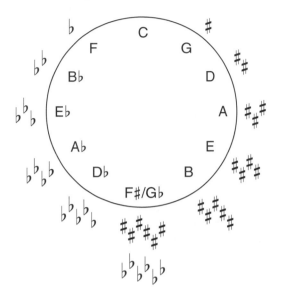

circuit bending. The customization of low-voltage, battery-driven electrical devices, such as toys and cheap synthesizers, to create novel musical instruments and sound generators.

circular bowing. A string technique in which the bow is kept in continuous motion by changing from down-bow to up-bow in a circular motion.

circular breathing. A wind instrument technique in which the performer breathes in through the nose while expelling air out through the mouth, thus creating a continuous sound.

circular canon. See perpetual canon.

Cl. Abbr. for clarinet.

clam. (1) A performance mistake. (2) To play an avoid note on a chord.

clarinet. A single-reed woodwind instrument.

clarsach. Celtic harp.

class compliant. A USB peripheral device that does not need drivers to work with a Mac or Windows PC.

classical guitar. A nylon-string acoustic guitar most often plucked by the fingernails of the nonfretting hand.

classical music. (1) Music written in the Western European art music tradition and utilizing standard acoustic ensembles. (2) A period in Western European art music spanning roughly from 1750 to 1825.

classic blues. Primarily acoustic blues music from the first half of the twentieth century.

Clav. Abbr. for clavinet.

claves. A pair of short hardwood or nylon sticks used as a percussion instrument.

clavichord. A soft-sounding keyboard instrument in which brass or iron strings are struck by metal tangents.

clavier. [Fr.]. Keyboard.

clavinet. An electronic version of a clavichord.

Clear Tone mute. See solo-tone mute.

clef. A symbol that is placed at the beginning of a staff and shows the pitch of written notes.

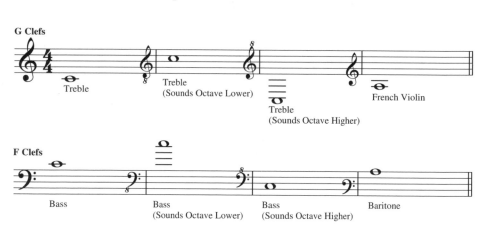

Percussion Clefs

Drum   Cymbal

Tablature

Guitar Tablature

click track. In audio recording, a metronome track that is fed into the headphones of a musician or group of musicians in order to keep precise time and aid in synchronization.

clip. (1) A small segment of audio or video. (2) Distortion caused by too high a level of an audio signal.

clipping. Harmonic distortion that occurs when an audio device is pressed to a level that is too high.

clock. A timing signal that synchronizes multiple digital devices.

close harmony. An arranging or performance technique in which the notes of a chord, usually other than the bass, are spaced with no chord member missing between consecutive voices.

closely related key. A key that is only one sharp or flat removed from the original key, therefore having many notes in common.

close miking. Placing a microphone near (usually within a foot of) a sound source in order to minimize sound from other sources.

close position. Where the notes of a chord, usually other than the bass, are spaced with no chord member missing between consecutive voices.

close structure. See close position.

closing credits. In a motion picture, television show, or video game, a list usually added at the end of the program naming the cast and crew, including the composer and/or music supervisor.

cluster. A group of notes, usually made up of half or whole steps, that sound simultaneously.

Cnt. Abbr. for cornet.

coaster. A CD-R that is useless due to a failed recording.

cocktail kit. A highly portable drum set that is played standing up and consists of a floor-tom-sized drum whose bottom head is played with a foot beater and top head is equipped with snares. Small cymbals and a pair of small attached tom toms are often part of the set.

coda [It.]. (1) Literally, tail. (2) The ending section of a piece.

codec. A computer program or device that is used to encode or decode a digital data stream.

codetta. A short section of music that concludes a larger section (often the exposition in a sonata) but is not the concluding section of a piece, per se. See also coda.

col [It.]. With the.

col legno [It.]. Play with the wood of the bow.

color. (1) A repeating pitch sequence in Medieval isorhythmic motets. (2) The overall sound of a piece. (3) A unique combination of instruments.

coloratura. An operatic vocal style that emphasizes trills, runs, leaps, and embellishments.

color coupling. In orchestration and arranging, the melodic pairing of two instruments from different instrumental families to create an unusual or unique timbre.

comb filter. A type of band pass filter that allows only the frequencies in multiple specified bands to pass through while attenuating or rejecting others. See band-pass filter.

combination tone. When a pair of notes are played very loudly, a note that is heard either above or below.

combinatorial. In serial music, a row and one of its transformations whose hexachords form the complete aggregate when combined.

combinatoriality. In dodecaphonic music composition, a condition wherein subsets of rows can be exchanged to create new rows.

combo. A small band or group of musicians playing a variety of instruments. Most often, a jazz or pop ensemble.

come [It.]. As, like.

come prima [It.]. As before.

comes. In counterpoint, the follower (answer).

come sopra [It.]. As above.

comma. The small interval that is the difference between a tempered interval of a fifth and one from the natural harmonic series. Also called a "Phythagorean" or "ditonic comma."

common chord. In harmonic analysis, a chord that is a member of two different keys. For example, F major is both the IV chord in the key of C major and the V chord in the key of B♭ major.

common practice period. An era in Western art music spanning roughly from 1600 to 1900, when music composition followed a shared method of harmony and counterpoint.

common time. 4/4 meter. Four beats to the bar.

comodo [It.]. Comfortably.

comp. (1) To play chords as an accompaniment. (2) To make a single track from many (composite).

complement. In set theory, the set of all notes (pitch classes) that are not in a given set; e.g., the complement of the C major scale (0, 2, 4, 5, 7, 9, 11) is the G♭ major pentatonic scale (1, 3, 6, 8, 10).

composer. A person who creates original music.

composite meter. A grouping of small metrical subunits into a larger whole; e.g., the time signature 3/8+2/8+3/8 used for a single bar or series of bars.

composite minor scale. A minor scale that blends two or more minor scales; e.g., C natural minor + C harmonic minor + C melodic minor creates C, D, E♭, F, G, A♭, A, B♭, B, C.

composite rhythm. The rhythm created by combining two or more rhythms; e.g., two dotted quarter notes combined with three quarters creates quarter, two eighths, quarter.

compound chord. A harmonic sonority created by stacking one chord on top of another; e.g., E major over C major creates C, E, G, G♯, B.

compound interval. A melodic or harmonic interval larger than an octave.

compound line. A single melody that implies two or more melodies.

compound melody. A single line that implies two or more lines.

compound meter. A time signature in which the beats in each measure are in subdivisions of three; e.g., 6/8, 9/8, 12/8.

compressed score. See reduced score.

compression. A signal processing technique in which the relative volume of loud sounds are reduced while the relative level of soft sounds are boosted.

compressor. An analog or digital device used in audio recording and broadcasting to reduce loud sounds and boost the volume of soft sounds, creating a more uniform overall loudness.

comp track. A recorded track that is a composite of the best sections of many takes.

con [It.]. With.

con brio [It.]. With vigor or spirit.

concert. A live music performance.

concert band. A large ensemble with sections of woodwinds, brass, and percussion.

concerted rhythm. In keyboard music, the simultaneous sounding of rhythms with both hands.

concert grand. A large piano, usually with a nine-foot, horizontal string case.

concertina. A small, hand-held, bellows-driven, free reed instrument with pitch buttons on both ends.

concertino. The small group of soloists in a concerto grosso.

concertmaster. (1) The performing leader of an orchestra or band. (2) The leader of the first violin section in an orchestra and the leader of the clarinet or oboe section in a symphonic or concert band.

concert music. See art music.

concerto. A composition for one or more solo instruments, accompanied by an orchestra or ensemble.

concerto grosso. A Baroque-period orchestra composition that pairs a group of soloists (concertino) with the full orchestra (ripieno).

concert pitch. (1) The actual sounds of notes, as opposed to the written pitches for transposing instruments. (2) The agreed-upon tuning pitch for an ensemble or orchestra. In modern international standard pitch, A4 is tuned to 440 Hz.

concert score. A music score in which all instrument parts are untransposed.

condensed score. A music score using a small number of staves, with multiple instruments represented on each staff.

condenser mic. A microphone that uses electricity and a capacitor to capture and amplify sound.

conductor. A person who leads an orchestra or ensemble.

confirming cadence. Following a modulation, a strong cadence that firmly establishes a new key.

conga. A tall, barrel-staved, single-headed drum of African origin that is usually played with the hands.

Congo Square. An open space in New Orleans where African slaves gathered to hold market, sing, play music, and dance in the eighteenth century.

conjunct motion. Stepwise melodic movement.

con licenza [It.]. With liberty.

connectivity. The number of inputs and outputs on audio, video, or computer gear, and their ability to be connected.

consequent phrase. (1) The second of two consecutive phrases that together may create a period. (2) The phrase that follows the antecedent phrase in a musical period.

conservatory. A school that provides a formal education in music. Many conservatories also have programs in dance and drama.

console. See mixing console.

consonance. (1) A chord, interval, or group of pitches that sound stable and/or do not sound harsh to most people. (2) A consonant interval.

consonant interval. The harmonic intervals of a perfect unison, major or minor third, a perfect fifth, a major or minor sixth, and a perfect octave.

consort. An ensemble of instruments of the Elizabethan period.

constant coupling. A mechanical voicing technique in big band writing and arranging in which the lead alto doubles the line of one of the trumpets, and the rest of the saxes follow the same contour.

constant structure. A series of three or more chords in which each chord is the same quality and type.

contact mic. A microphone that is attached to a surface and receives its input from the mechanical waves produced when the surface vibrates. Usually used for amplification or recording.

contemporary classical music. See art music.

contemporary folk music. An outgrowth of traditional folk music that was popularized in the mid-twentieth century. See also folk song.

contemporary music. Broadly, all music of the present time including rock, pop, classical, hip-hop, etc. See also art music.

contiguous dominants. Dominant chords whose roots move in a motion other than the typical descending perfect fifth or half step.

contiguous II Vs. Paired II Vs whose roots move in a motion other than the typical descending perfect fifth or half step.

continuo. See basso continuo.

continuous controller. A MIDI message device that can be used to send data to control volume, pitch bend, panning, and mod wheel. The device sends values from 0 to 127.

contour. The shape of a line or melody.

contrabass. (1) The lowest sounding member of the violin family. Standard tuning for the contrabass is E2, A2, D3, G3. (2) Below the bass.

contrabassoon. The lowest member of the bassoon family. Its range is B♭0 to A3 and is written an octave higher than it sounds.

contrabass saxophone. The lowest sounding member of the saxophone family, its standard range is D♭1 to A♭3. It is pitched in the key of E♭ and sounds two octaves and a major sixth lower than written.

contractor. A person who links music-industry work opportunities with musicians.

contrafagotto [It.]. Contrabassoon.

contralto. The lowest of the female classical voice types, typically with a range of F3 to F5.

contrary motion. In counterpoint, when one melodic line moves up while the other moves down.

contrasting period. A period in which the first and second phrases are different.

controller. A software or hardware device that sends MIDI data to another MIDI device.

control room. In a recording studio, a separate room that houses the recording console and is isolated from the performance space.

control surface. A digital audio workstation human interface device that gives the user tactile control of software.

control voltage. A predefined electrical signal sent to an analog device to change a parameter or trigger a response.

convolution. A mathematical operation on two functions that produces a modified result and is used in digital signal processing and computer music.

cool. See cool jazz.

cool jazz. A style of laid-back jazz that was a reaction to the complexity and fast tempos of bebop.

copyist. A person who prepares musical scores and parts.

copyright. The right to legal ownership of an original work and intellectual property.

cor anglais [Fr.]. See English horn.

corda [It.]. String.

CoreAudio. The audio subsystems of Mac OS X that handle audio communications between applications and the computer.

Corelli cadence. See Corelli clash.

Corelli clash. A phrase ending in which there are two consecutive dissonances prior to resolution, with the first sounding the root and second scale degree simultaneously, and the second sounding the root and leading tone simultaneously before resolving to tonic.

corksniffer. A person who debates the minute differences between and pros and cons of various products in order to find the perfect one.

cornet. A trumpet-like brass instrument only smaller, with a conical bore, and mellower tone.

corno [It.]. Horn.

corporate rock. See arena rock.

count. A spoken representation of the beat.

counterline. A secondary melody that contrasts with the primary melody.

counterpoint. The art, craft, and technique of setting two or more melodies simultaneously.

country and western music. A North American music style originating in the 1920s that mixes the spare instrumentation and simpler harmonies of country music with steel guitar, big band, and jazz influences.

country blues. A subgenre of country music that mixes African American blues music with acoustic country and folk music.

country music. A style of North American popular music with roots in the southern folk culture of the United States.

country rock. A subgenre of rock music that mixes rock music with country music.

country swing. A style of country-and-western music that features a walking swing bass line and swing eighths.

couplet. (1) Two rhymed lines of verse. (2) The contrasting sections of a rondo between the refrain.

coupling notes. Notes that are doubled (coupled) in constant or variable coupling.

course. A pair of strings tuned in unison or in octaves and played as a unit on a string instrument.

courtesy accidental. An accidental placed before a note to remind the player of an alteration or of the governing key signature.

cover. (1) A remake of a previously recorded song. (2) To perform another artist's song.

cover band. A group that primarily performs the music of other bands.

cowbell. A hollow, hand-held metal percussion instrument that is open at one end and is often played with a beater.

cowboy chord. See open chord.

cowboy music. See Western music.

CPS. Abbr. for cycles per second.

crab. Turntable technique creating a rapid burst of notes.

crab canon. A canon where the comes imitates the dux in retrograde motion.

crash cymbal(s). (1) A loud cymbal that is part of a drum kit and is intended for creating sharp accents. (2) A pair of cymbals that a percussionist uses to create loud accents and exclamations.

Cr. Cym. Abbr. for crash cymbals.

creative commons. A copyright that allows for free distribution of creative work.

critical listening. The art and technique of aural analysis of music's frequency response, dynamic range, tone, imaging, and instrumental blend.

croon. To sing or hum in a soft, flexible, sentimental fashion.

crooner. A popular singer who sings in a soft, sentimental style.

cross-coupling. A technique that connects the playback of one channel to the record of another channel on an analog tape recorder.

crossed voices. In polyphony, where a part that is usually lower (such as the tenor) moves above a part that is usually higher (such as the alto).

crossfade. (1) An audio-editing and DJing technique in which one part decreases in volume while another overlapping part increases in volume. (2) A digital music-editing technique in which one section decreases in volume while the next section increases in volume.

crossfader. A control on a DJ mixer that allows crossfades using a single fader control to mix two audio signals.

cross-harp. Second position on a diatonic harmonica. Often used for playing blues and rock music in which ♭3, ♭5, and ♭7 of the key are used.

crossover. Music that is popular in two genres at the same time.

crosspicking. A string-picking technique in which the plectrum (pick) jumps over a string.

cross relation. The chromatic contradiction of a note in one part by a note in another part.

cross-rhythm. See polyrhythm.

cross stick. A percussion technique in which a drumstick is laid across the head of a drum, extended over the rim, and strikes the rim with the side of the stick.

crosstalk. Signal bleeding from one channel to another in a multichannel audio system.

cross tuning. See scordatura or open tuning.

crotchet [Br.]. Quarter note.

crwth. A Welsh harp.

Csound. A computer-music application, originally written in the C programming language, in which the user can design sounds and software instruments and create a score file for realizing a composition.

Cubase. A professional-level digital recording, sequencing, editing, and mixing application (DAW).

cue. (1) The music in a scene or designated section of a film or media project. (2) A physical signal from a conductor that tells a performer that they are to play. (3) A marking on a score or part that shows a performer when to play.

cueing up. Setting up, preparing, and/or ordering music or film for play.

cue sheet. A document that provides detailed information about all of the music used in a film or television show.

cugaphone. Unconventional new-music instrument, often built by the composer, constructed from a brass mouthpiece, a flexible tube, and a funnel or bell.

cuica. A Brazilian single-headed friction drum.

cuivré [Fr.]. Brassy.

cup mute. A mute for brass instruments that removes both high and low frequencies, thus creating a focused and somewhat muffled tone.

cutaway score. A large ensemble score in which all staffs that do not include instrumental or vocal activity have been removed.

cutout score. See cutaway score.

cut scene. A linear section of a video game that is scored like a short film.

cut time. (1) Following the half note as the beat unit in 2/2 time. Also called alla breve and half time. (2) The meter signature for 2/2 time.

cutting. (1) A DJ or turntable technique to produce a short repeated sound. (2) Jamaican Maroon music rhythm. (3) The process of recording tracks. (4) The process of creating a vinyl record.

cutting contest. In jazz, an onstage playing competition that shows off instrumental virtuosity and musicality.

CWP. Contemporary Writing and Production, one of the departments in the Professional Writing and Music Technology Division at Berklee College of Music.

cycle 2. Chord root motion by seconds.

cycle 3. Chord root motion by thirds.

cycle 5. Chord root motion by fifths. Also, cycleV.

cyclic form. A form utilizing the repetition, or reintroduction and alteration, of earlier motivic or thematic material later in a musical composition.

Cym. Abbr. for cymbal.

cymbal. A percussion instrument made from a thin metal disk that is struck by a stick or other beater. Cymbals are often used in pairs and sounded by striking one against the other.

da capo [It.]. "The head," or beginning of a piece.

da, dal [It.]. From, by, for, of.

DAC. Abbr. for digital-to-analog converter.

dactylic. A strong rhythmic stress followed by two weak rhythmic stresses.

dada. An international art movement of the early twentieth century which challenged conventional standards and aesthetics.

daisy chain. (1) A series of connected devices, often used to connect MIDI devices. (2) To connect devices in a series.

Dalcroze Eurythmics. A method for music education developed by Swiss musician, composer, and educator Émile Jaques-Dalcroze, which emphasizes movement in addition to rhythm, structure, and expression.

dal segno [It.]. From the sign.

damper. A mechanical device on a piano that mutes the vibration of the strings.

Dampfer [Ger.]. A mute.

dance band. A musical combo that plays music mainly for dancing.

dancehall. Dub-influenced dance music developed in Jamaica in the early 1980s.

darkstep. A drum and bass subgenre featuring the chromatic scale and faster drum grooves.

DAT. Abbr. for digital audio tape.

DAW. Abbr. for digital audio workstation.

dB. Abbr. for decibel.

D&B. Drum and bass.

dbx. Audio noise-reduction systems that use a signal compression and expansion technique.

D.C. [It.]. Abbr. for da capo.

D.C. al Fine [It.]. Go back to the beginning and play until the fine (end) marking.

death metal. A subgenre of heavy metal music that features massive distortion, growling vocals, and ominous grooves.

decay time. In acoustics, the time it takes for a sound to become inaudible. Long decay times are associated with reverberant spaces.

deceptive cadence. A harmonic cadence that ends with the V chord moving to a chord other than I. Most often V VI or V ♭VI.

decibel. A sound pressure level (loudness) unit of measure.

decidé [Fr.]. Decided.

deciso [It.]. Decided.

deejay. See DJ.

de-essor. An audio device, such as a plug-in, that attenuates or eliminates excessive sibilant consonants from a recording or track.

dehors [Fr.]. Without; out of.

delay. (1) An audio signal that is recorded and repeated after a set duration of time. (2) A device that records and repeats an audio signal after a set duration of time. (3) The time it takes for a sound to travel through a device and to be heard. Often referred to as "latency."

delay compensation. A method for making up for signal latency.

delicate [It.]. Softly, delicately.

delta blues. An early form of blues originating in the Mississippi delta, often utilizing slide guitar, acoustic guitar, harmonica, and vocals.

demisemiquaver [Br.]. Thirty-second note.

demo. A preliminary recording of a song or piece of music that demonstrates the abilities of the performer or composer.

demo love. Preference of a demo recording over a produced recording.

density. (1) The close proximity of notes in a harmonic structure. (2) The quantity of simultaneous events in a piece of music.

depth. See bit depth.

derby. See hat mute.

dervish. See whirling dervish.

descant. (1) A melody that is to be sung above the primary melody and is higher in pitch. (2) A style of Medieval music in which a soloist singing a fixed melody is accompanied by one or more improvising singers.

descending cycle. A series of chords whose roots descend by step, by third, by fourth, or by fifth.

descending passing tone. A nonchord tone approached and left by step in a downward motion.

destructive editing. A digital editing process that overwrites existing information.

destructive recording. A digital recording process that overwrites existing information.

détaché [Fr.]. (1) Detached. (2) A string bowing technique alternating up- and down-bows and leaving a slight space between notes.

Detroit techno. Music that evolved from the techno music movement in Detroit in the 1980s and 1990s, often featuring drum machines and analog synths.

development. (1) The second large section of a classical sonata form in which the themes, rhythms, and harmonies presented in the exposition section are explored, embellished, and elaborated. (2) The elaboration of the thematic, harmonic, and rhythmic material of any composition.

Dha. The solfège syllable for the sixth note of an Indian scale.

dhrupad. The most unornamented form of classical Indian singing.

Di. The solfège syllable for a raised tonic (Do).

DI. See DI box.

diad. A two-note harmonic sonority (chord).

diamond. A notation mark in the Nashville number system indicating the rhythmic value of a whole note.

diamond record. A certification that an album or single has sold at least 10,000,000 units.

diapason. (1) An octave. (2) The main stop on a pipe organ. (3) A tuning device.

diatonic. Melody, chords, and harmonies derived solely from the heptatonic (major) scale or one of its modes.

diatonic scale. A heptatonic scale of the whole-step/half-step pattern W, W, H, W, W, W, H.

DI box. Abbr. for direct input box.

diddley bow. A homemade one-string instrument originating in the southern United States in the early twentieth century.

didgeridoo. An Australian wind instrument.

difference tone. See combination tone.

digital audio tape. A recording format invented by Sony in 1987 that recorded digital information on analog tape. Often referred to as DAT.

digital audio workstation. A computer-based system for recording, editing, mixing, and playing back music. Often referred to as a DAW.

Digital Performer. A professional-level digital recording, sequencing, editing, and mixing application (DAW).

digital piano. An electronic keyboard that uses digital samples of a piano as its sound source.

digital tape. An audio tape format in which digital information is recorded onto analog tape for storage and playback. See also digital audio tape (DAT).

dilruba. An Indian bowed stringed instrument with sympathetically vibrating strings. It is a cross between a sarangi and a sitar.

dim. (1) Abbr. for diminuendo. (2) Abbr. for diminished.

diminished. Reduced.

diminished approach. A diminished seventh chord or triad that moves stepwise to the root of a target chord or one of the target chord's chord tones from a half step above or below.

diminished interval. A minor or perfect interval that has been lowered by one half step.

Diminished Fifth

diminished seventh chord. A four-note chord that is constructed by stacking three minor thirds.

diminished scale. (1) One of the chord scales that accompanies a diminished seventh chord. (2) An octatonic scale. Also called a "whole-half scale." See Scales in the Appendix.

diminished triad. A three-note chord constructed by stacking two minor thirds.

diminuendo [It.]. Gradually becoming softer.

diminution. Intervallic or rhythmic contraction of a line.

direct box. See direct input box.

direct input box. In audio recording, a device used to connect a high-impedance signal to a low-impedance, balanced input.

direct modulation. A sudden change of key at the beginning of a phrase or new section.

director. See music director.

dirge. A mournful composition or funeral song in a slow tempo.

discant. See descant.

disco. A style of popular music with roots in European dance clubs in the 1970s, which often features a four-on-the-floor beat and a rhythmic electric bass part.

disjunct. Non-stepwise motion of lines; leaps.

disk drive. See hard drive.

dissonance. Two or more notes that, when sounded simultaneously, create a clash or incongruity.

dissonant interval. In traditional harmony, two tones forming a second, a seventh, or a tritone.

distantly related key. A key that is two or more sharps or flats removed from the original key and therefore shares fewer common tones.

distortion. (1) Compression of the peaks of a wave of an electrical signal, which produces a grainy or dirty sound. (2) An effect used by instrumentalists to add texture to a sound.

dithering. Adding noise to a digital audio signal to spread short-term errors across the audio spectrum.

ditone scale. A six-note scale of three successive half steps separated by a minor third (C, D♭, E, F, G♯, A).

ditonic comma. See comma.

ditty. A short song.

dive bomb. An electric guitar technique in which the vibrato (whammy) bar is pressed down while holding a note or chord to create a long downward pitch bend.

divisi [It.]. Divided.

dixieland. A style of New Orleans jazz music that arose in the early twentieth century.

DJ. (1) Variant of deejay. (2) A Jamaican musician who sings and talks (toasts) over an instrumental version of a song. See toaster.

djembe. A West African goblet-shaped, single-headed drum played with the hands.

Do. (1) The solfège syllable for the first scale degree. (2) The note C in fixed Do solfège.

dobro. An acoustic guitar with a metal resonator built into the body to amplify the sound.

docking station. A hardware stand into which a variety of computer, audio, and MIDI devices can be plugged in to receive power and/or be connected to one another.

dodecaphony. Twelve-tone serialism.

dog and pony show. Playing and presenting a cue to a film director.

dog ear. A single-coil guitar pickup with two flanges used to mount the pickup onto a guitar.

doghouse. (1) A raised patch bay on an audio mixer, with connections to its back panel, allowing the mixer to remain in its case. (2) An upright acoustic bass.

Doh. See Do.

doit. A notation mark telling the performer to perform a quick glissando upwards after playing the fundamental note. Most often used in jazz arranging.

Dolby. A noise-reduction method employed in audio recording and playback.

dolce [It.]. Sweetly.

dolcissimo [It.]. Very sweetly.

dolente [It.]. Sadly.

dolore [It.]. Grief.

doloroso [It.]. Sorrowfully.

dominant. (1) The fifth note of a major or minor scale. (2) A major or major-minor seventh chord built on the fifth degree of a major or minor scale. (3) A chord or note that has a similar function to the fifth note or major-minor seventh chord built on the fifth degree of a major or minor scale.

dominant pedal. Pedal point on the fifth degree of a key.

dongle. An electronic copy protection device that is inserted into a computer port to allow the user to run a software application.

doo-wop. A vocal style originating in the 1950s that features group vocal harmonies sung over a pop-influenced I VImi IV V R&B groove.

dope. Something exceptionally good.

doppio [It.]. Double.

doppio movimento [It.]. Twice as fast.

Doppler effect. The change in pitch (frequency) of a sound source caused by the contraction of approaching waves and rarefation of departing waves.

Dorian mode. (1) A Medieval church mode that can be represented by the white keys of a piano spanning D to D. (2) A modal minor scale constructed W, H, W, W, W, H, W. (3) A chord scale from the IImi7 of a major key. See Scales in the Appendix.

dot. A marking following a notehead that indicates the duration is one and a half times the duration of the note.

double. (1) To couple a melody line with a second instrument. See a2. (2) To play two or more instruments in a performance or recording.

double barline. Two vertical lines at the end of a measure, which denote a change of section, key, or time signature in a piece of music.

double bass. See contrabass.

double bassoon. See contrabassoon.

double chromatic approach. When a target note is approached by two different notes, each one a half step apart.

double flat. A notation symbol indicating a note is to be lowered by two half steps.

double harmonic minor scale. A harmonic minor scale with a raised fourth degree and a lowered second degree. See Scales in the Appendix.

double-lead. Having two lead players in a band or piece of music.

double neck. An electric guitar with two necks, with one usually being a twelve-string and the other a six-string.

double period. A period consisting of four phrases, of which the first three end with an inconclusive cadence and the fourth with a perfect authentic cadence.

double reed. A wind instrument with two opposing reeds that vibrate against one another.

double sharp. A notation symbol indicating that a note is to be played two half steps higher.

double stop. A string technique of playing two notes simultaneously.

double time. Twice the tempo of the written tempo.

double-time feel. Implying twice the tempo with a constant meter.

double tongue. A brass and woodwind technique for playing a pair or pairs of notes in rapid succession in which the player interrupts the airflow with the tongue to create two distinct attacks. Often taught as a "Ta-Ka" articulation.

douce [Fr.]. Soft.

douleur [Fr.]. Sorrow.

dovetailing. In orchestration, overlapping instruments to create a smooth line or transition.

downbeat. (1) The first beat of a measure. (2) The start of a performance.

DownBeat. A magazine about all things pertaining to jazz.

DownBeat **poll.** A list of the top jazz musicians according to *DownBeat* magazine.

down-bow. A bow stroke that starts at the frog of the bow and moves towards the tip.

download. (1) To transfer a file from one digital device to another. (2) A music file copied from the Internet.

DP. Abbr. for Digital Performer.

Dr. Abbr. for drum set.

drag. In turntable technique, a slow, drawn-out scratch.

dragging. Playing slower than the beat.

DRC. Dynamic range compression.

drift. Unintentional shift of frequency due to the inaccuracy of recording equipment.

drive. See disk drive.

driver. A software program that allows an operating system and other software to communicate with a hardware device.

dronal. Harmonically nonfunctional music that is organized around a single pedal tone (drone), in which the relationships are created between moving melodic lines.

drone. A sustained note or notes.

drop. (1) In a music track, a point where there is a significant change in arrangement, usually in the bass or rhythm. (2) A point in hip-hop and electronic music where both the bass and drums reenter.

drop 2. An arranging and playing technique for close-position seventh chords where the second from the highest chord member is played or written down an octave.

drop 2&3. An arranging and playing technique for close-position seventh chords where the chord members second and third from the top are played or written down an octave.

drop 2&4. An arranging and playing technique for close-position seventh chords where the chord members second and fourth from the top are played or written down an octave.

drop 3. An arranging and playing technique for close-position seventh chords where the chord member third from the top is played or written down an octave.

drop chord. A specifically arranged inverted chord. See drop 2, etc.

drop tuning. Lowering a string's tuning; e.g., lowering the sixth string (E2) of a guitar to a D2.

drum. A percussion instrument made with a hollow resonating body and one or two membranes that produce sound when struck.

drum and bass. A style of primarily electronic nightclub music developed in the 1990s featuring heavy bass and sub-bass along with prominent drums.

drum and bugle corps. A marching-band group that consists of a color guard, percussion section, and brass section.

drum corps. See drum and bugle corps.

drumline. The percussion section of marching bands.

drum machine. A sequencer or electronic instrument that is programmed to play samples of drums and other percussion instruments, often taking the place of a live drummer.

drum set. A kit of drums and cymbals made to be played by one person. The basic set consists of a bass drum, snare drum, one or more tom toms, floor tom, hi-hat cymbals, ride cymbal, and crash cymbal.

drumstick. A beater made from a tipped stick that is used to play drums and other percussion instruments.

drum throne. A stool that a drummer sits on.

dry. The absence of reverb or other signal processing.

D.S. [It.]. Abbr. for dal segno.

D.S. Abbr. for drum set in score notation.

D.S. al Coda [It.]. Performance direction to go to the sign and then to the coda.

DSP. Digital signal processing, a mathematical modification of an input signal.

dual function chord. A chord that can be analyzed as simultaneously having two functions;. e.g., IIImi7 V7/II II where the IIImi7 functions both as a nominal tonic and in a secondary-dominant relationship.

dub. (1) A genre of EDM and reggae music that evolved in the 1960s. The style features remixes (dubs) of preexisting recordings. (2) Short for overdub.

dub-hop. A mixture of dubstep and hip-hop music.

dub plate. Jamaican DJ language.

dub stage. A room where the final mix of a film or other visual media project is made. Overdubs and voiceovers are often done in this facility.

dubstep. An EDM music style that originated in London in the 1990s and has roots in dub, jungle, and reggae.

duduk. Armenian oboe.

dudy. Czech bagpipes.

duende. A transcendent quality assigned to the finest moments and artists in flamenco music.

duet. Music written for or performed by two players.

dulcimer. A fretted, wooden-boxed, multi-stringed instrument that is played by plucking the strings or by striking the strings with small hammers. See hammered dulcimer.

duo. Two performers.

duophonic. A mono recording that has been made into stereo by splitting the signal and applying processing techniques.

duple. Double.

duple meter. A two-beat measure.

dur [Ger.]. (1) Major. (2) Major key.

duty cycle. The percentage of time an electrical signal takes to perform an on-off cycle.

dux. In counterpoint, the leader or the subject of a fugue.

DX7. The first FM synthesizer. Marketed in the 1980s.

dyad. A two-note chord or interval.

dynamic mic. A microphone that uses a thin diaphragm to capture sound vibrations. The vibrations generate an audio signal through motion in a magnetic field.

dynamics. Indicating the loudness and softness of music or sounds.

e [It.]. And.

ear buds. A pair of small headphones that are inserted into a listener's ears.

ear candy. Particularly pleasing music and sounds.

ear training. See aural training.

ear worm. A melody or musical fragment that sticks with the listener.

E. Bs. Abbr. for electric bass.

E-Bow. A hand-held electronic device for an electric guitar that simulates the sound of bowing.

échappée [Fr.]. See escape tone.

echo chamber. (1) A room, space, or enclosure designed to be reverberant and used for recording. (2) An electronic device for simulating a large reverberant space.

Echoplex. A tape-delay effect machine invented in the late 1950s for use by guitarists and vocalists.

ECM feel. A spacious and esoteric jazz and new art music recording sound developed by Manfred Eicher's ECM record company.

EDM. Electronic dance music.

effects. Signal processing, such as reverb, distortion, phasing, and the like, which are added to an audio signal.

effects pedal. A foot pedal that allows a performer to switch rapidly between sounds.

effects unit. A stand-alone module containing effects such as reverb, distortion, chorusing, and so on, which can be utilized by various audio devices and instruments.

EG. Envelope generator.

egg shaker. A small oval percussion rattle filled with pellets.

E. Gtr. Abbr. for electric guitar.

Egyptian scale. See Scales in the Appendix.

E. Hrn. Abbr. for English horn.

eilend [Ger.]. Hurrying.

einfach [Ger.]. Unison.

elán [Fr.]. Verve.

electric bass. A bass guitar with electronic pickups.

electric blues. A genre of blues music in which the guitar, bass, vocals, drums, etc. are all amplified.

electric cello. A cello, often solid body, with an electronic pickup.

electric guitar. A guitar with electronic pickups.

electric piano. An electronic keyboard instrument that emulates the sound of an acoustic piano.

electric violin. A violin, often solid body, with an electronic pickup.

electro. Subgenre of EDM featuring drum machines and electronic sounds.

electroacoustic. Art music that combines electronic sound production with live performance or with samples from traditional acoustic instruments and sound sources.

electroclash. A style of music that combines EDM, techno, electro, and synthpop with an emphasis on songwriting and performance art.

electronic music. Music created by instruments and computers that use electronic technology and are not merely amplified by eletromechanical means.

electronic organ. A keyboard organ, such as Hammond, church, or home organ, that was originally made to imitate the sound of a pipe organ through electromechanical or digital means.

electrophone. A musical instrument powered by electricity.

elegante [It.]. With grace and style.

elegy. A funereal lament or mournful song or piece of music.

elevator music. A form of innocuous recorded music that is meant to be background music when holding on the phone, grocery shopping, eating in a restaurant, or riding in an elevator. Also known as "Muzak."

elision. Two phrases of music or text in which the ending of one phrase is the beginning of the next.

embellish. To ornament or decorate a melody or musical accompaniment.

embellishing dominant. A dominant chord used in a passing, neighboring, or other usually noncadential function.

embouchure. The positioning and shape of the lips and facial muscles when playing a brass or woodwind instrument.

Emmy. An award for excellence in the television industry, including excellence in musical composition.

emo. A style of rock music originating in the 1980s that features self-revelatory lyrics and expressive melodies.

emulation. Simulation of a physical audio device using audio modeling software.

encore. A piece of music played following the program in response to the audience appreciation for the program and demand for more.

end credits. See closing credits.

end pin. A stick at the base of a cello or bass that holds the body of the instrument off of the ground to facilitate playing it.

end title. The closing credits of a film, often accompanied by a lengthy music cue.

energico [It.]. Energetically.

engineer. See audio engineer.

English horn. A double reed woodwind instrument of the oboe family. The English horn is in the key of F, sounds a perfect fifth lower than the oboe, and has a range of E3 to C6.

enharmonic. A note, key signature, scale, or chord that sounds the same as another but is spelled differently; e.g., B♭ and A♯.

enharmonic scale. A nontempered scale in which typically enharmonic notes (e.g., D♭ and C♯) are not equivalent.

enigmatic scale. See Scales in the Appendix.

ensemble. A group of instrumentalists and/or singers.

ensemble figures. A melody and/or rhythmic line that is played simultaneously by a group of instruments and/or singers.

entr'acte [Fr.]. (1) An intermission between the acts of a musical or opera. (2) Music that is played between the acts of a musical or opera.

envelope. The shape of a sound over time. Typically showing the amplitude of a sound's parameters including the attack, decay, sustain, and release (ADSR).

EPD. Electronic Production and Design, one of the departments in the Professional Writing and Music Technology Division at Berklee College of Music.

E. Pno. Abbr. for electric piano.

EQ. Abbr. for equalization.

equalization. In recording or playback, the mixing, balancing, enhancing, or reducing of specific frequencies of an audio signal.

equalizer. An electronic or digital device that balances, enhances, or reduces specific frequencies of an audio signal.

equal temperament. A tuning method in which the octave is divided into twelve equal parts so that adjacent pairs of notes have a similar ratio.

erhu. A two-stringed, bowed instrument used in traditional Chinese music.

escape tone. A nonharmonic tone that is approached by step and resolved by a leap.

escolas de samba [Port.]. Brazilian samba schools and performing ensembles.

espressivo [It.]. With expression.

étude. A musical study composed for the development of a specific technique.

etwas [Ger.]. Somewhat.

euphonium. A mellow-sounding, conical-bore brass instrument with a range of F1 to F5.

Eurodisco. A form of electronic dance music that was an outgrowth of disco music in Europe in the 1970s. Pop, rock, and English-language vocals are additional influences.

Eurorack. A chassis that houses a set of small modular synthesizers that often come in do-it-yourself project kits.

eurythmics. See Dalcroze Eurythmics.

evensong. Prayer that is sung in the evening in the Anglican Church liturgy.

event list. An index of all MIDI messages sent and received in a MIDI sequencer.

execution. An instrumentalist's or vocalist's technical performance and interpretation of music.

expander. A digital or analog device that increases the differences in dynamic range of an audio signal. The opposite of a compressor.

exposition. The opening section of a fugue or sonata in which the thematic materials for the composition are introduced.

expression. (1) A MIDI continuous controller command that allows for the modulation of sounds over time. (2) Performing with variations in loudness, tempo, attack, and timbre to create a colorful soundscape.

expressionism. A Western art-music style from about 1910 to 1930 in which anxious and emotional moods were depicted in music that was often atonal.

expression mark. A performance direction in a score or part.

extemporize. To improvise music on the spot.

extended dominants. A string of three or more dominant chords that start on a strong harmonic stress point and whose roots move down in perfect fifths, minor seconds, or a combination of the two.

external clock. A timing source that sends timing information from outside of a primary sequencer, synth, drum machine, or other device to synchronize them.

external sync. A parameter on a sequencer, synth, drum machine, or device that synchronizes to an outside clock source.

Fa. (1) The solfège syllable for the fourth degree of a major or minor scale. (2) The note F in fixed Do solfège.

facilmente [It.]. With ease.

fade. To gradually reduce in volume.

fader. A volume control (variable attenuator), most often found on a mixer, which slides forward and back, rather than being turned like a knob.

fado. Melancholic music usually for singer and guitar, which originated in the 1820s in Portugal.

fagotto [It.]. Bassoon.

Fairchild compressor. A classic vacuum tube compressor built by the Fairchild company in the 1960s.

Fairlight CMI synthesizer. An early digital sampling synthesizer (computer music instrument) designed by the Fairlight company in 1979 in Australia.

fake book. A lead-sheet compilation of jazz tunes, pop tunes, and standards.

fall. A downward drop from a specific note to an indefinite ending pitch. A technique often used in big band jazz arranging.

false harmonic. See artificial harmonics.

false relation. See cross relation.

falsetto. The range that is just above a singer's modal range.

fandango. A lively Spanish dance in triple meter.

fanfare. A short musical flourish, usually played by brass and percussion, often used to announce an important person or event.

Fantasie [Ger.]. A free-form composition with an improvisational character.

Farfisa organ. A compact, portable electronic organ made by the Italian Farfisa company in the 1960s. It was part of the signature rock/pop sound of the 1960s.

fasola. See shape note.

fatback. A heavy, slightly delayed backbeat on beats 2 and 4. Often used in soul and funk music.

fauxbourdon [Fr.]. A fifteenth-century French contrapuntal technique in which the plainsong melody is transposed up an octave and harmonized at the sixth below. By the Classical period, this was a designation for progressions based on parallel sixth chords.

f clef. On a staff, a notation element that indicates the line where the note F3 is located. Most commonly, bass clef.

Fe. In solfège, the fourth degree of the scale lowered by one half step.

feedback. The squealing noise created by a feedback loop in an amplification system.

feedback loop. A condition created by adding the output of a signal into the input signal, thus creating a recursive loop.

feel. A combination of style, groove, mood, and ambience of a song or composition.

feminine cadence. A harmonic cadence that ends on a beat that is normally unaccented.

Fem. Vox. Abbr. for female vocalist(s).

Fender. A musical instrument company that makes guitars, basses, amplifiers, and music accessories.

Fender bass. A widely used electric bass guitar first marketed by the Fender company in 1951.

Fender Rhodes. An electric piano invented by Harold Rhodes and first marketed by the Fender company in 1965. The piano uses metal tines connected to amplified tonebars that are struck by hammers.

Fender Twin Reverb. A classic tube guitar amplifier featuring two twelve-inch speakers. The Fender Twin was first marketed by the Fender company in 1952.

fermata. A notational mark indicating that a note or rest is to be prolonged. Also called a "bird's eye" or a "bull's eye."

feroce [It.]. Ferociously.

FFT. Fast Fourier Transform, an algorithm for transforming a function of time into a function of frequency.

f-holes. The two f-shaped openings on the face of a violin, viola, cello, bass, some guitars, and other stringed instruments.

Fi. The solfège syllable indicating the raised fourth degree of a major or minor scale.

Fibonacci series. A series of numbers, beginning with 0 and 1, in which the following number is generated from adding the two previous numbers. (0, 1, 1, 2, 3, 5, 8, 13, 21, etc.).

field drum. A drum to which a harness has been added so that it can be used when marching.

field holler. Antebellum African American vocal music related to work songs. Often cited as a precursor to the blues.

fife. A small, wooden, transverse flute of narrow bore with a shrill tone. It originated in Medieval Europe and is often used in military and marching bands.

fifth. (1) The interval between five diatonic notes. (2) A chord tone five diatonic notes above the root.

fifth motive. Using the fifth of a chord as an embellishing note.

figured bass. A music notation system developed in about 1600 that uses numbers and symbols to indicate intervals to be played above given bass notes.

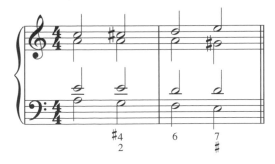

fill. A short musical improvisation used to fill in the gaps between phrases or sections in a song or arrangement.

filk. A folk-music genre originating in the United States in the 1950s that features science-fiction themes.

filter. An electronic or digital device used to attenuate signal level within specific frequency ranges.

finale. The closing section of instrumental work, often grand in nature.

Finale. A widely used computer-based graphic notation application.

finalize. The last step in preparing a CD for play.

final mix. A recording of a song or composition that is complete and ready for mastering.

fine cut. A film that has been edited and is now locked.

Fing. Cym. Abbr. for finger cymbals.

fingerboard. A flat surface on the neck of a string instrument where a player's fingers depress the strings to create pitches.

finger cymbals. A pair of small cymbals of Turkish origin, which are attached to the fingers and often played while dancing.

fingering. The choice of which finger to use to play notes on an instrument.

finger pick. (1) A guitar pick used for finger-style guitar playing. (2) To play guitar in fingerstyle.

finger rest. A short bar that is placed above or below the strings of a guitar, bass, or mandolin. When below, the four fingers rest on it while the strings are plucked with the thumb; when above, the thumb rests and the four lower fingers pluck the strings. Also known as a "thumb rest."

fingerstyle. A guitar technique in which the individual fingers, with or without finger picks, are used to pluck the strings.

fipple flute. An end-blown woodwind with a constricted mouthpiece and windcutter. Recorders and penny whistles are of this family.

FireWire. A high-speed serial connection.

five-string bass. An electric or acoustic bass with five strings, rather than the usual four. The fifth string either lowers the possible range (B0, E1, A1, D2, G2) or raises it (E1, A1, D2, G2, C3). The higher tuning is often referred to as "tenor tuning."

fivetissimo. A dynamic marking, used to please film directors, when a situation requires the music to be significantly louder than fortissimo.

fixed Do. A solfège system in which "Do" is always the note C, regardless of key.

Fl. Abbr. for flute.

flag. An appendage on a note that indicates the note value. Functionally similar to a beam, but used for unbeamed notes. One flag = eighth note, two flags = sixteenth note, three flags = thirty-second note, etc.

flageolet. A string harmonic.

flam. A two-note percussion technique in which a very short grace note is played before the second note.

flamenco. Spanish music and dance from Andalusia, characterized by highly rhythmic guitar playing, dancing, handclaps, and singing.

flamenco guitar. See classical guitar.

flanger. A device or plug-in that processes a signal using delay and modulation to create a rich tone.

flash drive. A digital storage device that is typically inserted into a USB drive.

flat. (1) A notation symbol that when placed in front of a note indicates that the note is to be lowered by one half-step. (2) When a singer or instrumentalist is singing or playing under the pitch.

♭

flat-four beat. With all four beats accented evenly in 4/4 time.

flatpicking. Guitar and other string instrument technique in which a plectrum (pick) is used to strum or pluck the strings individually.

flat-top guitar. A guitar whose top (soundboard) is flat rather than convex (as on a violin).

flatwound. A string for a guitar, or other string instrument, that has a flat wire wrapped around a core.

flexatone. A hand-held percussion instrument consisting of a small metal leaf that is struck with a beater, creating a high-pitched metallic glissando.

Flgl. Abbr. for flugelhorn.

flicker noise. See pink noise.

flip. In jazz arranging or performance, an upward glissando from a starting pitch to a neighboring tone or indefinite pitch, followed by a downward glissando to a target note.

floating bridge. A bridge that is held in place by the tension of the strings rather than being anchored to the top face of a guitar or other string instrument.

floor tom. A low-sounding, three-legged, double-headed drum that is part of a standard drum set (kit).

flugelhorn. A brass instrument, similar in shape to a trumpet, with a wide, conical bore that gives it a mellower tone than that of a trumpet.

flute. (1) An edge-blown aerophone instrument of the woodwind family. (2) The modern Western concert flute, an edge-blown transverse flute with a fingering mechanism that covers holes to change pitches.

flutter. In a tape-recording system, fast variations (more than 5 Hz) brought on by fluctuations in the transport system.

flutter tongue. A tonguing technique used in wind instrument playing to create a whirring sound.

FM radio. A radio format adopted in the United States and other countries in 1961, which utilized frequency modulation and allowed for high-fidelity stereo broadcast of music.

FM synthesis. A music synthesis technique that utilizes frequency modulation to create complex waves from sine tones.

FOH. Abbr. for front of house.

Foley. The process of creating and synchronizing acted-out sound effects for film and television, named after sound-effect editor Jack Foley.

folklorico. Traditional folk music of Spain.

folk music. See folk song.

folk rock. A style of music that evolved during the 1960s and blended elements of rock music with folk music.

folk song. A simple traditional song, often by an unknown composer, that is transmitted aurally.

follower. (1) The imitating voice (comes) in contrapuntal music. (2) A person who subscribes to another's Twitter or other social media feed.

footballs. Whole notes.

footwork. A dance style associated with house music.

foreground. (1) In arranging, music that is to stand out; e.g., the main theme. (2) In Schenkerian analysis, the exterior structure of the music.

formant. Frequency band of acoustic resonance or spectrum in a human voice or resonator.

forro. Brazilian music style.

forte [It.]. Loudly.

fortepiano. A predecessor of the modern piano that got its name from its ability to play both loudly (forte) and softly (piano).

found sound. Sounds that occur in the world that are incorporated into a composition. Often associated with musique concrete, tape music, and electroacoustic music.

Fourier transform. In digital signal processing, the decomposition into frequency components of a complex sound wave.

four note. See shape note.

four on the floor. Bass drum beats on every beat (1, 2, 3, 4) in common (4/4) time.

fourth. The interval between four diatonic notes.

four-way close. Chords, usually seventh chords, where the notes of a chord are spaced with no chord member missing between consecutive voices.

foxtrot. A popular twentieth-century American couples' dance that is in a medium 4/4 tempo.

fractal. A self-similar object that regenerates at succeedingly smaller and larger levels.

frame drum. A drum with the drumhead stretched across a shallow frame instead of a larger resonating chamber.

frame rate. The number of frames that go by in one second (or other predetermined duration) of film or video.

frat boy. A style of hip-hop and rap made to appeal primarily to high school and college-age listeners.

free counterpoint. Counterpoint that does not follow the processes and rules of strict counterpoint.

free improvisation. Playing without a predetermined form, tonal center, or harmony.

free jazz. Improvised jazz music that does not rely on chord progressions, melodies, or forms and is created on the spot.

free reed. A frame-held reed that vibrates without an opposing surface.

free stroke. See tirando.

free time. To conduct and synchronize a film cue to picture without a click track or punches and streamers.

free tone. A nonchord tone that is approached by leap and resolved by leap.

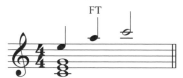

French horn. A mellow-toned valved brass instrument with two sets of tubing and a narrow bore. The modern horn transposes at the fifth and has a range of F♯2 to C6.

French overture. An overture, popularized in eighteenth-century France, with the form of slow-fast-slow.

French sixth chord. A four-note chord with an augmented sixth between the outer voices, and with a major third and augmented fourth from the bottom note forming the inner voices.

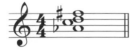

French violin clef. A treble clef with the scroll (G4) placed on the bottom line of a staff.

frequency response. The span of frequencies a loudspeaker or audio component can reproduce.

fretboard. See fingerboard.

freudig [Ger.]. Joyfully.

frevo. Brazilian music style.

Fr. Hrn. Abbr. for French horn.

fröhlich [Ger.]. Happy.

front of house. (1) The audience portion of a theater or concert hall. (2) When a mixing or recording console is situated in the audience rather than on the side of a stage.

frottola. A popular form of choral music in sixteenth-century Italy.

fuga [It.]. Fugue.

fugato [It.]. An imitative contrapuntal composition or musical section in the style of a fugue but not adhering to the strict process of fugal composition.

fugue. A contrapuntal compositional process in which a theme (subject) is presented, imitated at a different pitch, and then developed.

full dominant cadence. See perfect authentic cadence.

full jazz cadence. A harmonic cadence that ends IImi7 V7 I.

full score. The entire score of a musical composition that shows all instruments at all times whether they are playing or not.

fully diminished seventh chord. In traditional harmony, a seventh chord that has both a diminished fifth and seventh.

function. The role an individual chord plays in functional harmony.

functional harmony. In tonal music, the concept that each chord has a specific role in moving the music forward. The three primary categories are: tonic, subdominant, and dominant.

functional motive. A motive that outlines the harmony.

fundamental. The lowest tone of a harmonic series.

funk. A musical style that emerged in the 1960s, blending elements of soul and R&B. The music features syncopated sixteenth-note grooves in the bass and drums.

funky. Exhibiting the characteristics of funk music.

fusion. (1) Music that is a blend of jazz and rock. (2) Any blend of different styles or genres of music.

Futurama. A brand of electric guitar from the 1950s. Best known for being one of George Harrison's earliest electric guitars.

futurism. A style of early twentieth-century music that embraced the experimental use of mechanical sounds and nontraditional instruments.

fuzz box. A device that distorts an electrical signal to the point that it nearly becomes a square wave, thus creating complex overtones.

fuzz tone. See fuzz box.

FX. Abbr. for sound effects.

G. Abbr. for gong.

Ga. The solfège syllable for the third note of an Indian scale.

gagaku. Traditional Japanese court music.

gain. (1) The amount of amplification. (2) The knob or fader that controls the amount of amplification.

gain stage. Any point in an audio recording or playback system where the level of signal flow can be adjusted.

gain staging. Adjusting the signal flow levels to avoid distortion and noise.

gamba. An instrument of the viol family. See viol and viola da gamba.

gamelan. A mostly metallophone ensemble of percussion instruments originating from Bali or Java.

gamut. The entire group of solfège syllables from low to high (Ut, Re, Mi, Fa, Sol, La, Ti, Ut).

gangsta. A style of urban rap and hip-hop that raps about urban violence and crime.

gang vocals. A group of singers recorded to simulate the sound of a crowd sing-along at a concert.

garage band. An amateur or semiprofessional band that usually plays simple, rough-hewn rock music and rehearses in the family garage, basement, or other nonprofessional rehearsal space.

GarageBand. A music recording, editing, and sequencing program.

garage rock. (1) Originating in the 1960s, a style of rock and roll that is unsophisticated and raw. (2) The music that amateur bands play in their garages or similar nonprofessional rehearsal spaces.

gate. In synthesizers and audio recording devices, an analog or digital device that allows certain signals and/or elements to pass through.

gato. Argentinian folk music for dancing, often featuring humorous lyrics.

gauge. The measure of the diameter of a string.

gavotte. A Renaissance French folk dance in moderate 4/4 meter.

GB. Abbr. for general business music, a collection of light popular music songs mixed with jazz standards.

GB gig. A musical engagement in which the band is expected to play light popular music and possibly some jazz standards.

gear. All forms of equipment for music making and recording.

gender. Bronze Indonesian xylophone with resonating chambers under the bars.

General MIDI. The standardized MIDI specification that allows many digital instruments to communicate by responding to MIDI messages.

German sixth chord. A four-note chord that is built with a major third, perfect fifth, and augmented sixth from its root.

GESAC. European Grouping of Societies of Authors and Composers. A rights society representing thirty-four of the largest authors' societies in the European Union, Norway, and Switzerland.

Gesamkunstwerk [Ger.]. An art work in which the composer controls all of its aspects.

gesture. A physical or mental movement that adds nuance and direction to a musical phrase.

ghaita. Oboe-like shawm.

ghatam. A clay pot used as a percussion instrument in South Indian classical music.

ghazal. Light Indian classical music song style.

ghost note. A note that has a definite rhythmic value but an indefinite pitch.

gig. A musical engagement or job.

gig bag. A soft-cover carrying case for a musical instrument.

gigue. A lively dance in 6/8 time popularized in seventeenth-century Europe.

giocoso [It.]. Joyful, playful.

glam. A style of rock music from the early 1970s that featured performers in glittery costumes, platform shoes, and heavy makeup.

glass harmonica. A musical instrument that features revolving glass bowls of graduated sizes that together create a scale. The bowls are played with moistened fingertips.

glee. An unaccompanied song from the English Baroque of three or more parts.

glissando [It.]. A performance technique in which a note is approached from above or below by gliding from the starting to the ending pitch.

glitch. (1) A purposeful sound of a skip or other imperfection in a piece of electronic or digital music. See also stutter. (2) A style of music from the late 1990s that features skips, imperfections, and other purposefully introduced noises.

glitter rock. See glam.

Glock. Abbr. for glockenspiel.

glockenspiel. A high-pitched percussion instrument that is constructed of metal bars laid out in keyboard fashion and played with mallets.

GM. See General MIDI.

gobo. A sound-absorbing panel that is placed so as to isolate the sound of an instrument in a recording studio.

gold record. A certification that an album or single has sold at least 500,000 units.

gong. A large, plate-shaped, bronze percussion instrument of Indonesian origin, which is suspended from a frame and struck with a mallet.

gooseneck. A bendable, flexible microphone stand adapter.

gospel music. A genre of praise music in the Christian Church.

goth. (1) A rock style with roots in the late-1970s British punk scene, characterized by dark, gloomy lyrics and music. (2) A follower of goth music and culture.

gothic rock. See goth.

GP. See grand pause.

grace note. An ornamental note often added before a note of longer duration.

GRAMMY. (1) An award given by the National Academy of Recording Arts and Sciences for notable music industry achievement. The term comes from the award's initial name: "Gramophone Award."

gran casa [It.]. (1) A large two-headed drum. (2) Bass drum.

grand pause. A break in the music usually indicated by a fermata, caesura, or GP marking.

grand piano. A large piano with a horizontal string case measuring from five to ten feet in length. See also baby grand and concert grand.

grand rights. Permissions to use music, negotiated among producers, publishers, and copyright holders, to stage an opera, musical theater production, or play.

grand staff. A pair of staves, one treble clef, and one bass clef, connected by a brace.

graphic editor. A digital music editor that allows the user to manipulate visual elements of a music score or of a mix.

graphic equalizer. An analog or digital equalizer that has sliders to control the relative level of frequency bands.

graphic score. A music score that includes visual representations instead of traditional musical notation and symbols.

grave [It.]. Slowly.

grazioso [It.]. Gracefully.

great Highland bagpipes. Bagpipes of Scottish origin.

Gregorian chant. Unaccompanied monophonic plainchant of the Catholic Church attributed to Pope St. Gregory (540–604 C.E.).

grille cloth. The fabric stretched across the face of an amplifier or loudspeaker.

griot. An African musician, praise singer, storyteller, and poet.

groove. The continuous rhythmic pattern used in songs to establish style and feel.

ground. See ground bass.

ground bass. A repeating bass pattern over which variations in harmony and melody may be played.

ground lift. A sound-recording technique used to attenuate or eliminate hum and noise by interrupting ground loops.

growl. (1) A style of singing in death metal that utilizes a deep, raspy, throat voice. (2) The technique of singing into the mouthpiece of a woodwind or brass instrument to create a raspy, guttural effect.

grunge. An alternative rock style that emerged in the 1980s and features distorted guitars and edgy vocals.

Gtr. Abbr. for guitar.

guajeo [Sp.]. In Cuban music, an arpeggiated-chord ostinato pattern.

GUI. Abbr. for graphic user interface.

guide tone. A note from a guide-tone line.

guide-tone line. A smooth, linear melody created from the chords' thirds and sevenths to clarify a chord progression.

Guidonian hand. A graphic image of a human hand with solfège syllables drawn on the fingers. It was attributed to Guido d'Arezzo (990 to 1050) and used as an aid for memorizing the scale degrees.

guiro. A Latin American gourd-shaped percussion instrument that has notches cut from the sides and is played by scraping a stick across the ridges.

guitar. A six-stringed instrument with a long fretted neck attached to a resonating chamber or a solid body. The strings are plucked or strummed with the fingers or a pick. The typical range is from E2 to B5, with the upper note dependent on the length of the neck.

guitarron. A large, deep-toned guitar often used in mariachi and Latin music.

guitorgan. An electric guitar outfitted with organ-like tone generators that are triggered by pressing frets on the fingerboard.

gypsy jazz. A style of swing jazz whose development is attributed to the 1930s French Romani guitarist Django Reinhardt.

gypsy minor scale. A natural minor scale with a raised fourth. See Scales in the Appendix.

gypsy picking. A rest-stroke style of picking attributed to the 1930s French Romani guitarist Django Reinhardt, that creates a bigger sound and more speed.

Haas effect. See precedence effect.

hairpin. A decrescendo or crescendo marking.

half cadence. A harmonic cadence that ends on a V chord.

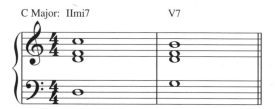

half diminished. A seventh chord constructed from a diminished triad and a minor seventh. It is a diatonic seventh chord built on the seventh degree of a major scale.

half note. An open notehead with a stem that gets two beats in 4/4 time.

half rest. A rest held for the duration of two quarter rests, written as a short, filled-in rectangle sitting on a line of a staff.

half step. The interval between two adjacent notes in a chromatic scale.

half-step minor-third scale. See Scales in the Appendix.

half time. See alla breve.

half track. An analog tape recorder with a recording head that records two tracks, each on one half of the tape.

half-whole scale. An octatonic scale and diminished scale. See Scales in the Appendix.

halling. A lively Norwegian folk dance in 2/4 meter.

hammer. The mechanical device that strikes the string of a piano or other instrument when a key is depressed, causing the string to sound.

hammered dulcimer. A wooden-boxed stringed instrument that is played by striking the strings with small hammers.

hammering. Performing hammer-ons.

hammer-on. The technique of playing a stringed instrument by striking the string on the fretboard, usually with the fretting hand, for a percussive effect.

Hammond B-3 organ. An electronic organ with two keyboards and a set of foot pedals created by American inventor and engineer Laurens Hammond in the 1930s. The Hammond B-3 sound is often associated with gospel music, jazz, rock, and blues.

hanabera. A popular Cuban dance of the nineteenth century built on a 2/4 rhythm of dotted eighth and sixteenth notes, followed by two eighth notes. Also called "Cuban contradance."

handle. Extra music before or after the body of a film music cue that can be used in editing if needed.

hand organ. See street organ.

Hardanger fiddle. Norwegian fiddle with four drone strings.

hard bop. A style of bebop music from the 1950s with elements of R&B, blues, and gospel music.

hard core. A fast and heavy offshoot of punk music that originated in the 1970s.

hard disk. A digital storage disk that can store large quantities of data.

hard-disk recording. A digital recording method in which the digital information is recorded directly to a rigid disk data-storage device.

hard drive. The mechanism that controls the functioning of a hard disk in a computer or off-board device.

hard rock. A subgenre of rock music developed in the 1970s, featuring distorted guitars and aggressive drums and vocals.

hardstep. A drum and bass subgenre featuring grittier bass lines.

harmonic. (1) An overtone that is an integer multiple of the fundamental. (2) A note produced on a string instrument by lightly touching a node (such as the fifth, seventh, or twelfth fret on a guitar).

harmonica. A small, usually rectangular, mouth-blown wind instrument with many small chambers, each with a free reed.

harmonic major scale. See Scales in the Appendix.

harmonic minor scale. A natural minor scale with a raised seventh. See Scales in the Appendix.

harmonic phrase. A series of chords that ends with a cadence.

harmonic rhythm. The rhythm created by the changing chords in a progression.

harmonic series. The sequential set of overtones that are multiples of a fundamental frequency.

harmonium. A keyboard reed organ that is made to sound by foot-pumped bellows. Also called a "pump organ."

harmonizer. A device that splits an input signal so one or more of the split signals can be set to sound a harmony (usually a third or fifth) above or below the original signal.

Harmon mute. A wah-wah mute for brass instruments made by the Harmon company.

harmony. (1) The sounding of two or more pitches (notes) at the same time. (2) The underlying chord structure of a piece of music. (3) Additional parts that accompany a melody.

harp. (1) A framed, multistringed instrument with a perpendicular soundboard that is plucked with the fingers. (2) Name for a harmonica or blues harp.

harpoon. A harmonica or blues harp.

harpsichord. A stringed keyboard instrument originating in the fifteenth century, played by plucking the strings with quills or hard pieces of leather.

Harry Fox Agency. A company that specializes in collecting and distributing mechanical license fees on behalf of music publishers.

hat mute. Originally, a bowler hat used as a brass mute. Now, most are constructed from synthetic materials.

Haupstimme [Ger.]. Main (top) part.

hautbois [Fr.]. Oboe.

hautbois d'amour [Fr.]. See oboe d'amore.

Hawaiian guitar. See steel guitar.

Hawaiian slack key. A style of playing guitar that originated in Hawaii and utilizes various open tunings and fingerpicking. Also known as "slack key guitar."

HD. See hard drive.

head. (1) The melody of a tune. (2) The main body of a tune containing the primary melody and chords of a song. (3) A drumhead.

headphone mix. In a recording studio or session, the track mix given to a performer. This usually emphasizes the performer's track and other tracks that will aid the performer while recording.

headphones. A pair of small loudspeakers that are placed in or over a listener's ears.

head voice. The highest register of the voice, with vibration occurring in the head.

heartland rock. A subgenre of American rock music that originated in the Midwest in the 1970s and is characterized by earnest music and working-class lyrics.

heavy metal. A style of rock music that emerged in the 1970s, featuring loud, distorted guitars, driving bass and drums, and an overall dense sound.

heckelphone. A double-reed instrument pitched an octave lower than the oboe.

helicon. A large circular-shaped brass instrument of the tuba family.

hemidemisemiquaver [Br.]. Sixty-fourth note.

hemiola. (1) Two notes in the span of three or three notes in the span of two. (2) Two bars of music in triple meter played as if there were three bars of duple meter.

hepcat. A jazz musician, beatnik, or 1940s hipster.

heptatonic scale. A seven-note scale.

hertz. A measure of wave frequency in which each unit (1 Hz) is one cycle per second.

heteronomous music. Performance music that utilizes games and strategy to produce conflicting sounds and indeterminate results.

heterophonic. Referring to a music texture created by simultaneous variations of a single melody.

hexachord. (1) A six-note set of pitches. (2) The six Guidonian solmization syllables: Ut, Re, Mi, Fa, So, La.

hexad. A six-note chord.

hexatonic. A six-note scale.

HH. Abbr. for hi-hat.

hidden fifths. In common-practice voice leading, separate lines that move in similar motion into perfect fifths, thus interrupting the flow of independent-sounding voices.

hidden octaves. In common-practice voice leading, separate lines that move in similar motion into perfect octaves, thus interrupting the flow of independent-sounding voices.

hi-fi. (1) Short for high fidelity recordings that are engineered for high-quality reproduction of sound. (2) Home stereo system.

high impedance. See impedance.

high life. A musical style that emerged from Ghana in the early twentieth century and features a bell part similar to the Cuban claves.

high-pass filter. An analog or digital device that allows only frequencies above a specified range to pass through while attenuating or rejecting those below.

hi-hat. See hi-hat cymbals.

hi-hat cymbals. Two cymbals placed on a stand with one on top of the other, which move up and down through the use of a foot pedal. Typically, they are part of a drum set.

hillbilly boogie. Combination of African American boogie-woogie rhythms and country music.

hillbilly music. Rural music of the southern United States with its roots in bluegrass, old-time, and country-and-western music.

Hindu scale. See Scales in the Appendix.

Hindustani music. North Indian classical music.

hip-hop. A musical style originating in late twentieth-century African American culture and featuring stylized rhythms, rapping, sampling, scratching, and DJ'ing.

historical musicology. The study of music composition, performance, criticism, and reception ranging from the past to the present.

hit. (1) Accent. See also kicks. (2) A very popular piece of music. (3) The start of a gig.

Hn. Abbr. for horn.

hocket. Two or more musical lines combined to create a single melody.

Höfner bass. A violin-shaped electric bass popularized by Beatles member Paul McCartney. Also know as a "Beatle bass."

hollow body. An electric guitar with the body shape and open cavity of an acoustic guitar.

homophonic. Music in which the notes of the chords move in the same rhythm.

honky-tonk. (1) A bar where music is performed for customers often either by solo pianists or by country bands. (2) A style of rhythmic barroom piano music.

hook. A catchy musical idea often found in the chorus of a song.

hootenany. A folk-music gathering in which musicians play for each other in front of an audience.

horn. (1) French horn. (2) Any wind instrument; e.g., saxophone, trumpet, clarinet.

horn section. (1) The group of saxophone and brass instruments in an R&B or soul band. (2) The group of French horns in an orchestra or concert band.

hot. A high-level audio signal.

house. A style of electronic dance music from 1980s Chicago, featuring four-on-the-floor kick drum beats and repetitive rhythms.

house sync. A synchronization signal supplied to all of the devices in a recording or project studio.

Hp. Abbr. for harp.

Hpscd. Abbr. for harpsichord.

humanize. A processing technique in MIDI sequenced music that adds and subtracts small increments of time to the note and rhythm values to make them sound more like they were played by human beings.

humbucker pickup. An electric guitar and bass pickup that uses two coils to cancel out interference and noise, and to reduce hum.

Hungarian minor scale. See Scales in the Appendix.

hurdy-gurdy. A droning stringed instrument played by a wheel.

hybrid chord. A chord formed by playing a triad or seventh chord over a bass note that is not part of the upper-structure chord. These types of chords often create a tonally ambiguous sound, and on lead sheets, are notated as slash chords.

hybrid score. A film or other media score that is a mix of acoustic music and digitally produced music.

hybrid voicing. The interval construction of a hybrid chord.

hypermeter. A large-scale meter in which the individual measures are analogous to beats in a measure.

hypo modes. In the church modes (also known as the "Gregorian modes"), a mode such as Dorian whose primary tessitura explored the notes a fourth below the final.

Hz. Abbr. for hertz.

ictus. The point of a beat; downbeat.

Ictus. A jazz fusion band founded by Dave Mash in the 1970s.

idée fixe [Fr.]. Literally, fixed idea. A recurring theme that serves as a structural foundation of a piece of music.

idiophone. A musical instrument that depends on the material out of which it is made for the creation of its sounds. Idiophones include cymbals, wood blocks, thumb pianos, and the like.

IDM. Abbr. for intelligent dance music.

idyl. A composition with a calm and charming character.

IFPI. International Federation of the Phonographic Industry, an organization representing the recording industry worldwide.

ijexá [Port.]. A rhythm pattern from northeastern Brazil that is often used in popular Brazilian music.

iMIDI. A freeware application that allows software to connect and communicate like a rewire, but transfers MIDI data instead of audio signals.

imitation. A contrapuntal technique in which a melody is repeated by another voice or voices at the same or a different pitch level.

immer [Ger.]. Always.

impedance. The measurement of resistance level, in ohms, of a circuit. Components with low impedance will allow more current to flow through them than ones that are high impedance.

implied harmony. Harmony that is heard through the shape and stresses of a solo melody or in polyphony.

implied melody. A melody that emerges through notes emphasized in the harmony.

impressionism. A Western classical music style popularized by French composers Claude Debussy, Maurice Ravel, and others in the early twentieth century.

improvisation. Creating music in real time in a set form, over chord changes, or without a preconceived stylistic, rhythmic, or harmonic foundation.

incidental music. Music written for a play or other media presentation that is not primarily musical in nature.

incomplete subdominant cadence. A harmonic cadence that ends on IVMa7 or IImi7.

indeterminacy. A compositional and performance technique that utilizes chance elements. See also stochastic music.

indirect resolution. In harmony, when resolution to a target chord is interrupted by the insertion of its related II chord.

industrial dance music. A subgenre of electronic dance music that features heavy electronic beats, soaring keyboard melodies, and sampled vocals.

industrial metal. A music style that mixes metal music with industrial dance music.

industrial music. (1) A 1970s music style that mixes rock, punk, and electronic music infused with mechanical sounds and rhythms. (2) An avant-garde music style that features noise and controversial topics.

industrial rock. A music style that blends rock music with industrial music.

infrasonic. Frequencies below the range of normal hearing.

inharmonic. (1) An overtone that is not part of the harmonic series. (2) Not harmonic.

in head. The opening melody of a jazz tune played before solos are taken.

inner form. Formal musical structures that are nested inside the larger form of a piece of music.

inner hearing. The capacity for hearing music in our mind without relying on outside sounds. Also known as "audiation."

input. An electrical receptor or digital gate that allows an audio signal to enter.

input gain. A control knob or fader that allows a signal to be amplified.

insert. A mixing-board circuit that allows external devices to be added into the signal between the preamplifier and the mix bus.

instrumentation. (1) The choice of instruments in a musical arrangement. (2) The study of musical instruments.

instrument choir. A group of similar instruments.

intellectual property. Creations of the mind, including literary and artistic works that are used in commerce. Copyright law protects these creations.

intelligent dance music. An offshoot of electronic dance music that focuses on experimentation and individuality. Also called "art techno."

interface. A software or hardware connector between two devices.

interleaved. An audio file-management system that stores all channel information in an alternating single stream.

interleaved stereo. A single file that has the digital data for both stereo channels.

interlude. A short piece of music that is inserted between larger sections of a composition. Also referred to as "intermezzo."

intermezzo. (1) A short piece of music that is inserted between larger sections of a composition. (2) A short musical character piece.

international standard pitch. An agreed-upon standard tuning of A4 = 440 Hz.

Internet protocol address. A unique number assigned to a device in a computer network. An address may include the Internet service provider's and organization's name, and the IP's host name, country, region/state, city, latitude and longitude, and area code.

interpolated chord. A chord of short duration, placed between a dominant approach chord and a target chord. The interpolated chord usually has a minor seventh or a V7sus4 quality.

interrupting chord. See interpolated chord.

interval coupling. A harmonization between two parts in which the harmonizing interval remains constant; e.g., parallel fourths.

in the box. (1) Digital music that is performed solely by a computer. (2) Improvising in jazz and other music styles using only notes from the basic chord scales.

intonation. (1) The accuracy of a performer's pitch. (2) The opening pitch sequence in Gregorian chant.

intoning. Singing the opening pitches in a Gregorian chant.

intrada [It.]. An introduction or prelude to a composition in late-Renaissance and Baroque music.

intro. Abbr. for introduction.

introduction. The opening of a song or composition.

invariance. In set theory, two sets with common pitch classes.

invention. A short, imitative keyboard composition in two parts.

inversion. (1) The reversal of the order of an interval created by putting the lower pitch above the higher or vice versa. (2) The placement of a chord tone, other than the root, as the lowest note of a chord.

invertible counterpoint. A contrapuntal technique in which the higher voice becomes the lower voice while still adhering to correct stylistic principles.

I/O. Short for input/output.

Ionian. (1) The first of the church modes with the same interval construction as the major scale. (2) The chord scale for a tonic major chord. See Scales in the Appendix.

iOS. Internet operating system, an operating system for mobile devices.

IP. (1) Intellectual property. (2) Internet protocol.

IP address. See Internet protocol address.

iPod. A portable, personal music and media device.

Irish Mixolydian. Similar to the Mixolydian church mode, a major scale with a lowered seventh degree.

Irish whistle. See tin whistle.

ISCM. International Society for Contemporary Music.

iso booth. See isolation booth.

isolation booth. A small soundproof room, usually connected to a control room and part of a larger studio complex, used for recording soft or loud instruments that may otherwise experience bleed from other instruments or bleed into other microphones.

isorhythm. A Medieval composition device in which a repeating rhythm occurs throughout a piece or section.

istesso tempo [It.]. In the same tempo.

Italian sixth chord. A three-note chord that is built with a major third (usually doubled in four-part harmony) and augmented sixth from its root.

jack. (1) The audio plug on electric guitars, other musical instruments, and audio devices used to connect them to amplifiers and other audio equipment. (2) A rectangular piece of wood with an attached plectrum that moves up and down to pluck a harpsichord string.

jacking. A dance style associated with house music.

Jackson. A brand of electric guitar made famous by heavy-metal guitarist Randy Rhoads.

jaleo [Sp.]. A vocal encouragement to flamenco dancers as they perform.

jam. (1) To improvise over chord changes. (2) To participate in a session that includes improvisation (especially in jazz). (3) A piece of music or song.

jam band. A music group that utilizes extended improvisations in their performances.

jams. Songs.

jam session. A musical get-together in which improvisation is a primary focus.

Japanese scale. See Scales in the Appendix.

Javenese scale. See Scales in the Appendix.

jaw harp. A plucked metal idiophone that uses the mouth as a resonating chamber. Also known as a "Jew's harp" or "mouth harp."

JAZ cartridge. A hard-disk digital storage device.

jazz. A uniquely American music genre that blends African rhythms, forms, sounds, and melodies with European harmonies and relies extensively on improvisation.

jazz half cadence. A harmonic cadence that ends IImi7 V7.

jazz minor scale. An ascending melodic minor scale. See Scales in the Appendix.

jazz standard. A popular song that is part of the repertoire of jazz bands.

jazz waltz. A jazz tune in 3/4 time.

jeté [Fr.]. A "thrown" rebounding, bouncing bow stroke in string playing.

Jew's harp. See jaw harp.

jig. A folk dance in a brisk 6/8 or 12/8 meter.

jit. A fast, driving, percussive dance music of Zimbabwe.

jitter. Short for MAX/MSP/Jitter, a set of matrix data-processing objects optimized for video and 3-D graphics.

jive. (1) A 1930s American ballroom dancing style, which is a variation on the jitterbug and is based on African American dance. (2) South African term for popular music.

joik. An improvised Sami (indigenous Lapp) song.

jota. Traditional dance music of Northern Spain most often in 3/4 meter.

J-pop. Japanese popular music.

jubilee. Celebration and celebratory music and dance associated with the Jewish religion and later the Christian Church.

jubilees. Spirituals.

jug-band music. An early twentieth-century southern U.S. musical genre featuring clay jugs used as wind instruments, along with a mix of other instruments made from household items such as washtubs and washboards. Traditional instruments such as the banjo, fiddle, and guitar were also often part of the ensemble.

juju. A style of Nigerian popular music with roots in Yoruba percussion.

jump blues. A style of fast-tempo blues popular in the 1940s, played by small combos with horns.

jump-up. A drum and bass subgenre featuring robotic bass and heavy sounds.

jungle. An electronic dance music genre featuring drums and percussion. Also called "oldskool jungle," or "drum and bass."

just intonation. Using just tuning as the basis for intonation.

just tuning. A tuning system based on the overtone series that uses intervals of the fifth (3:2 ratio) and major third (5:4 ratio).

kantele. Finnish zither-like folk instrument with at least five to more than forty strings.

kantrum. Cambodian popular music style.

karaoke. A form of entertainment that involves singing to recordings of popular music hits from which the main vocal line has been removed.

karnatak. South Indian classical music.

kaval. Long wooden Bulgarian rim-blown flute.

kazoo. A small metal or plastic wind instrument that is played by humming into the mouthpiece to create a buzzing vocal sound.

Kbd. Abbr. for keyboard.

kettledrum. See timpani.

key. The root note, primary scale, and derived harmonies of a piece of tonal music.

key area. The tonal region of a piece of music.

keyboard. (1) A musical instrument of the piano or organ family. (2) An electronic or digital synthesizer. (3) A set of depressible bars that are laid out horizontally in representation of the twelve-note tempered scale.

keynote. The first tone (tonic) of a scale or key.

key of the moment. A key that is implied when a diatonic major or minor triad, other than the tonic, is preceded by its dominant chord (a secondary dominant).

key signature. A notation element on a music staff that shows how many sharps or flats are in a music composition, thus indicating the key.

KH-relation. In set theory when a set (group of pitches) is a subset of another set and of its complement.

kick drum. A bass drum played by a foot pedal with a beater. Typically part of a drum set (kit).

kicks. Rhythmic accents played by the rhythm section.

kicks over time. Accents played over a steady beat.

Kirnberger tuning. A temperament (tuning system) created by eighteenth-century composer and theorist Johann Kirnberger.

kirtan. Call-and-response chanted music, often accompanied by instruments and used for meditation.

kit. A drum set.

kithara. A box-shaped ancient Greek string instrument, similar to a large lyre.

Klang [Ger.]. Sound, tone.

Klangfarbe [Ger.]. Tone color.

Klangfarbenmelodie [Ger.]. Tone-color melody.

klavier. (1) Any keyboard instrument. (2) A stringed instrument with a keyboard. See also clavier.

klavier. A piano other than a grand piano.

klezmer. A musical genre rooted in the music of the Ashkenazi Jews of Eastern Europe. Much of the repertoire consists of dance and instrumental tunes.

knee. In an audio compressor, the shape of the response curve angle created by the ratio of the output level to the input level.

Kodály method. A technique for teaching children music developed by Hungarian composer and educator Zoltán Kodály in 1925. The technique includes teaching rhythm and movement, hand-sign solfège syllables, rhythmic solfège syllables, moveable Do solfège, and the use of high-quality age-appropriate music literature.

Kontakt. A digital sample library, sampler and sample editor

kora. Multistringed traditional Malian instrument.

koto. Japanese stringed instrument.

K-pop. Korean popular music.

K-relation. In set theory, when a set (or group of pitches) is a subset of another set or of its complement.

kriti. South Indian religious music form.

Kyrie. A prayer in the Christian liturgy, often set to music.

kwitra. See quitra.

La. (1) The solfège syllable for the sixth note of the major scale (a major sixth above the tonic). (2) The note A in fixed Do solfège.

laid-back. (1) Relaxed. (2). Having a relaxed groove created by playing slightly after the ictus of a beat.

laissez vibrer [Fr.]. Let it vibrate.

lament. A song of mourning.

lamisgroovitis. A player's inability to play a solid groove.

langsam [Ger.]. Slow.

la pompe. A percussive two-beat guitar picking pattern used in Gypsy jazz.

lap steel guitar. A variant of a steel guitar, played on the lap with a metal slide instead of depressing the strings with fingers. It is often tuned to a chord, in contrast to typical guitar tuning.

largo [It.]. Slowly.

laryngologist. A medical doctor who specializes in working with the voice.

latency. Delay in a system between an initial stimulus and a response.

Latin. A general designation for South American and Caribbean style music. Straight eighth notes and syncopated rhythms are implied.

layered event. In a composition, when contrasting, and sometimes unrelated, material, possibly in differing meters, is played by different instruments or instrument groups.

layered ostinato. In a composition, when repeating lines occur simultaneously in more than one musical voice; e.g., in the bass and in the soprano.

lay out. To refrain from comping.

Ld. Vox. Abbr. for lead vocalist(s).

Le. The solfège syllable for a lowered sixth note of the major scale (a minor sixth above the tonic).

lead. (1) Melody notes in a lead sheet. (2) The top note of a chord voicing.

lead guitar. The guitar part in a band that plays solos and often single-line melodies.

leading tone. The seventh degree of a scale, a half step below the tonic, that has a tendency to resolve up to tonic.

leading whole-tone scale. See Scales in the Appendix.

lead line. In jazz and pop arranging, the main melody of a musical arrangement that is harmonized underneath by the other brass and wind instruments. Usually the top voice is played by the lead trumpet player.

lead sheet. A notated reduction of a song that includes the melody, chords, lyrics, and basic form.

lead singer. A vocalist who sings the primary melody and lyrics in a band or musical group.

lead trumpet. The trumpet that plays the top part in a jazz band or pop ensemble.

leaning tone. A nonharmonic tone that is approached by a leap and resolved downward by step. Also called an "appogiatura."

leap. In voice leading and in melody analysis, consecutive melodic movement upward or downward by an interval larger than a whole or half step.

ledger line. A short horizontal line that extends the staff above or below its normal five lines.

legato [It.]. Smoothly, in a connected fashion.

leggiero [It.]. Lightly.

legitimate music. See art music.

legit music. See art music.

leitmotif. A musical motto or phrase that is associated with a person, place, thing, idea, or emotion.

lento [It.]. Slowly.

Leslie speaker. A rotating speaker inside a wooden cabinet. Often associated with the Hammond B-3 organ.

Les Paul. A solid-body electric guitar named after guitarist and artistic consultant Les Paul and sold by the Gibson guitar company. The guitar has been the instrument of choice of many influential guitarists including Jimmy Page, Joe Perry, Keith Richards, and others.

LFO. Low frequency oscillator, an electronic or digital device that produces a repeating pulse below 20 Hz.

L.H. Abbr. for left hand.

Li. The solfège syllable representing the raised sixth degree of a major scale (an augmented sixth above the tonic).

library music. Generic music that is written for various situations and moods and is part of a collection licensed for use in media productions. See also music library.

lick. A short, catchy musical phrase. The term is used mostly in jazz, pop, and rock music.

lickin' stick. Clarinet.

licorice stick. Clarinet.

Lied [Ger.]. Song, usually an art song.

Lieder [Ger.]. The plural of lied.

ligature. (1) A device that holds the mouthpiece onto the body of a woodwind instrument. (2) A Medieval notational symbol indicating that two or more notes are to be played. (3) A tie linking one note to the next.

Lightpipe. An optical ADAT transmission cable.

limiter. An audio compression device that prevents gain above a user-set threshold.

line cliché. A commonly heard melodic line within a chord progression.

line in. An audio signal input that is made to accept line-level signals.

line level. An audio signal of +4 dBu in professional audio or −10 dBV in consumer audio, as opposed to weaker signal levels of microphones and guitar pickups.

line out. An audio signal output that is made to send line-level signals.

line writing. A method of jazz arranging that focuses on the linear motion of voices between target chords as opposed to simply connecting vertical sonorities. The method was developed and taught by Berklee professor Herb Pomeroy.

lining out. A technique, primarily in gospel music, of embellishing a melody, usually by a vocal soloist, in a choir setting.

lip. In brass playing, to change the pitch of a note by using the lips rather than a valve.

lip sync. To give the impression of live singing by moving the lips in synchronization with a prerecorded piece of music or vocal track.

lip trill. In brass playing, to use the lips rather than the valves to alternate the pitches of a trill.

l'istesso tempo [It.]. The same tempo.

liuto cantabile [It.]. (1) Literally, singing lute. (2) A five-course, modern mandolin-like instrument combining registers of bass and tenor range: C2, G2, D3, A4, E4.

locked picture. In movie and visual media production, when all edits and changes have been completed and the product is ready for audio mixing and online editing. Also known as "picture lock."

lock in. To play in the same tempo and groove with another player or players.

loco [It.]. (1) Literally, in place. (2) Play as written.

Locrian mode. (1) The seventh mode of a major scale that is constructed H, W, W, H, W, W, W. (2) A chord scale from the VIImi7♭5 of a major scale. See Scales in the Appendix.

Locrian natural scale. See Scales in the Appendix.

lo-fi. (1) A mixing technique in which the low and high frequencies are attenuated in order to give a recording a retro sound. (2) Poor (low) quality sound.

lofting. A dance style associated with house music.

log drum. A rectangular wooden or bamboo box-shaped resonating percussion instrument, often with multiple slits. When struck, it produces pitches and is not a true drum, but an idiophone. Also called a "slit drum."

Logic. A professional-level digital recording, sequencing, editing, and mixing application (DAW).

Logic Pro. See Logic.

Lollapalooza. A yearly music festival that presents the top acts in popular music.

longa. In Medieval European mensural notation, a note value equal to four whole notes.

looper. A digital music device that records and plays back loops. See also looping.

looping. (1) A digital music technique that records a predetermined length of music or sound and repeats it. (2) A music performance style/technique in which musical arrangements are created in real time by playing, recording, and then layering loops.

lossy compression. A data encoding compression scheme that excludes information deemed to be unnecessary.

loud pedal. The sustaining pedal on a modern piano.

loudspeaker. A transducer that produces sound by converting electrical energy into an audible signal.

lounge gig. A musical engagement in a low-end bar or tavern, which usually involves playing light, popular GB music.

louré [Fr.]. Gentle and connected bowing technique on a bowed string instrument.

lower neighbor. In melodic analysis, a note that moves a step or half step below a chord tone and then returns to the chord tone.

low impedance. See impedance.

low-interval limit. In arranging and orchestration, the lowest and smallest interval between two adjacent voices to assure clarity in a voicing.

low-pass filter. An analog or digital device that only allows frequencies below a specified range to pass through while attenuating or rejecting those above.

LP. (1) Abbr. for long playing. (2) A vinyl record rotating at 33 1/3 revolutions per minute. Considered long playing in comparison with 45 RPM and 78 RPM formats. (3) Abbr. for Logic Pro.

lunga [It.]. Long.

lustig [Ger.]. Merry.

lute. A plucked, necked, wooden, multi-course string instrument that is related to the oud and is a predecessor of the guitar.

luthier. A maker and/or repairer of stringed instruments.

l.v. Abbr. for laissez vibrer.

Lydian ♭7 scale. A Lydian scale (mode) with a lowered seventh degree. See Scales in the Appendix.

Lydian ♯2 scale. See Scales in the Appendix.

Lydian augmented scale. See Scales in the Appendix.

Lydian chord. A major 7(♯11) chord.

Lydian minor scale. See Scales in the Appendix.

Lydian mode. (1) A Medieval church mode that can be represented by the white keys of a piano spanning F to F. (2) A modal major scale constructed W, W, W, H, W, W, H. (3) A chord scale from the IVMa7 of a major key. See Scales in the Appendix.

lyre. (1) An ancient Greek U-shaped, plucked string instrument. (2) An attachment on a marching instrument that holds notated music.

lyrical. In a singing fashion.

lyrics. The words to a song or vocal composition.

ma [It.]. But.

Ma. The Indian solfège syllable for the fourth note of a scale.

madrigal. A three- to eight-part Renaissance vocal composition, usually sung a cappella and featuring secular lyrics.

maestoso [It.]. Majestically.

magic square. See matrix.

magnetic tape. Recording tape used by reel-to-reel tape recorders.

mainstream jazz. A designation for 1950s jazz that stuck to an older swing big band feel rather than the bebop style that was popular at the time.

main title. In film scoring, a musical introduction to the main body of a movie. Similar to an overture in opera.

major. Pertaining to the major scale, major chord, major key, or major triad.

major chord. A chord whose lower three notes form a major triad.

major key. A tonal area whose primary notes and chords are from a major scale.

major Locrian scale. See Scales in the Appendix.

major pentatonic scale. See Scales in the Appendix.

major scale. A heptatonic scale constructed W, W, H, W, W, W, H, as in the Ionian mode. See Scales in the Appendix.

major triad. A three-note chord constructed with a major third and perfect fifth above the root.

Malagueña. (1) Spanish folk music of the provinces of Malaga and Murcia. (2) A genre of Venezuelan folk music. (3) A 1928 popular song by Cuban composer Ernesto Lecuona.

Male Vox. Abbr. for male vocalist(s).

mallet. A percussion beater with a large head made from yarn, felt, plastic, wood, or metal.

mambo. A Cuban dance and music style similar to the cha-cha and rumba.

manager. An administrator who handles the booking and representation of a musician, band, composer, or arranger.

mandocello. A low member of the mandolin family, with four courses of strings tuned C2, G2, D3, A3, similar to a cello.

mandola. A larger, mandolin-like instrument, with four courses of double strings, in alto (C3, G3, D4, A4) or tenor (G3, D4, A4, E4) tunings.

mandolin. A plucked or strummed fretted instrument with four courses of strings tuned in fifths with the individual pairs tuned in unison: G2, D3, A4, E4.

mandolino. A string instrument with four courses of double strings; an early predecessor of the mandolin, in various tunings.

Mannheim crescendo. An orchestration technique developed in Mannheim, Germany, in the mid-1700s, which adds sections of the orchestra, one at a time, to build the dynamic and musical energy level to a crescendo.

Mannheim rocket. An orchestration technique developed in Mannheim, Germany, in the mid-1700s, in which a rapidly rising arpeggio is orchestrated to move from the basses to the first violins and woodwinds.

ma non troppo [It.]. But not too much.

mano sinistra [It.]. Left hand.

manual. One of the keyboards of an organ or harpsichord.

manufactured chords. Chords that are not diatonic to any chord scale or usual harmonic system.

Maqam. An Arabic scale or mode, which is assigned a mood or season.

Mar. (1) Abbr. for marimba. (2) Abbr. for maracas.

maracas. Hand-held percussion instruments made from gourds or hollow wooden shells filled with seeds or pellets and are shaken to produce sound.

maracatú. A Brazilian music style.

marcato [It.]. Marked, accented, short.

march. Music, typically in a duple or quadruple meter, used for marching.

marching band. An ensemble made up primarily of brass, woodwind, and percussion instruments, sometimes supplemented by nonmarching instrumentalists, which performs at outdoor events.

mariachi. (1) A Mexican folk music style that is played by ensembles consisting of violins, trumpets, guitars, and voices. (2) A musician in a mariachi ensemble.

marimba. A percussion instrument constructed from pitched wooden bars with metal resonators underneath. The bars are laid out like a keyboard and struck with mallets.

Markov chain. A mathematical process that uses random variables and is sometimes employed in creating stochastic music.

mark tree. See bar chimes.

Maroon music. Music of escaped slaves, known as "Maroons" in Jamaica.

Marshall Stack. A powerful guitar amplifier from the Marshall company that has separate speaker cabinets (one or more) and an amp head. The amplifier of choice for many heavy metal and rock bands.

martellato [It.]. Hammered bowing.

marziale [It.]. In a military style, march-like.

mashup. A mix of two or more recordings to create a new complementary song or composition.

mass. (1) The celebration of the Eucharist. (2) A musical setting of certain parts of the Eucharist.

mässig [Ger.]. Moderate.

master. (1) The original finished recording of a song or album, usable as a template for replication. (2) In electronic and computer music, a controlling device or application. (3) To balance and to sonically shape the completed and mixed tracks of a recording or set of recordings (e.g., a CD) for clarity, consistency, and overall sound.

matrix. In twelve-tone serial music, a rectangle with 144 (twelve columns with twelve rows) inner squares that house all of the versions (prime, retrograde, inversion, retrograde inversion) of a twelve-tone row.

MAX. See MAX/MSP.

maximizer. A digital audio processor that increases the apparent loudness and presence of mix.

MAX/MSP. An object-oriented programming language for creating computer music and multimedia. MSP stands for MAX Signal Processing.

MBC. MIDI beat clock. See also MIDI clock.

mbira. An African thumb piano with tines that are attached to a hollow box and are plucked with the thumbs.

Me. The solfège syllable for the third note of a minor scale or lowered third of a major scale.

mean-tone temperament. A musical tuning system that utilizes the tempered fifth to generate the intervals.

measure. See bar.

mechanical royalty. A payment made to songwriters and composers when a copy of their music is made (pressed).

mechanical voicing. A voicing of a chord using a predetermined process such as drop-2.

mediant. (1) The third note of a scale. (2) A chord built on the third note of a scale.

Medieval. Referring to the Middle Ages in Europe, a period from approximately 500 to 1400.

Medieval folk. A musical style that emulates the sounds of Medieval European folk music through the use of period instruments and song forms.

Medieval folk rock. A musical genre from the 1970s that blends the sounds of Medieval folk music with modern song forms and is played on guitars, drums, and other typical rock instruments.

medley. A collection of songs or compositions played as a group, usually without pause.

melisma. Many notes sung using one syllable.

Go - ing up.

mellophone. A three-valved brass instrument often used in marching bands in place of French horns.

Mellotron. An electronic keyboard instrument invented in the 1960s on which keys trigger playback of strips of magnetic tape that have prerecorded sounds on them.

melodica. A free-reed mouth organ with a small piano-like keyboard. Also known as a "pianica."

melodic minor scale. A minor scale using the raised sixth and seventh scale degrees when ascending and the lowered seventh and sixth degrees when descending.

melody. (1) A series of individual notes that create the musical equivalent of phrases and sentences. (2) A tune.

melodyne. Digital audio-editing software that is used primarily for pitch correction.

membranophone. A musical instrument that creates sound through the vibration of a membrane; e.g., drums, string drums, and the like.

Memphis horn sound. The signature sound created by the horn section on many of the classic Stax records.

meno [It.]. Less.

meno mosso [It.]. Less motion.

mensuration canon. A canon in which one or more of the imitating voices imitates at a different speed. Also known as a "prolation canon."

mento. An acoustic Jamaican folk music played on a mix of African and European instruments. A precursor to ska and reggae.

merengue. A style of music in a fast 2/4 meter from the Dominican Republic.

Mersey Beat. A pop and rock music newspaper covering the Liverpool music scene in the 1960s.

Merseybeat. A rock and pop music sound that evolved from Liverpool and areas around the Mersey River in the early 1960s.

metal. See heavy metal.

metallophone. A percussion instrument made from pitched metal bars that are attached to a frame and played with mallets.

meter. The division of music into measures (bars), each with a certain number of beats.

metrical stress. (1) Beats in music that are regularly accented, thus creating meter; e.g., strong-weak-weak, strong-weak-weak creating 3/4 time. (2) The beats commonly stressed in certain time signatures; e.g., beats one and three in classical 4/4 time.

metric modulation. A note value from a prior measure that takes on a new note value in the ensuing measure; e.g., old dotted quarter = new quarter.

metronome. A device that gives an audible pulse or click in constant beats per minute. Often used by musicians for practicing or to synchronize music and players for recording.

mezzo [It.]. (1) Half, moderately. (2) Abbr. for mezzo soprano.

mezzo forte [It.]. Moderately loud.

mezzo piano [It.]. Moderately soft.

mezzo soprano. A female voice with a range between an alto and a soprano.

mezzo-soprano clef. One of the moveable C clefs where middle C is indicated on the second line of the staff.

mf. A dynamic indication for mezzo forte, or somewhat loud.

Mi. (1) The solfège syllable for the third degree of a major scale. (2) The note E in fixed Do solfège.

mic in. Abbr. for microphone input.

Mickey Mousing. Scoring a film or video project to very closely mirror the on-screen action.

mic pre. Abbr. for microphone preamp.

microphone. A transducer that converts sound into an electrical signal.

microphone preamp. A device designed to boost the signal strength of a microphone while not degrading the original signal quality.

microtonal. Music with intervals that are less than a half step.

microtone. An interval that is less than a half step.

middle C. The note C in the center of a piano keyboard vibrating at 261.6 Hz. Indicated as C4.

middle eight. An eight-bar contrasting section in a pop tune, typically occurring after verse I, chorus I, verse II, and chorus II have been played. Also referred to as a "bridge."

MIDI. Musical Instrument Digital Interface, a software and hardware protocol developed in the 1980s for connecting electronic music instruments, such as keyboards and sound modules, and computers with each other.

MIDI clock. A timing signal that is broadcast in beats per minute and synchronizes multiple MIDI devices.

MIDI interface. A hardware and software component that connects MIDI instruments, modules, and computers with one another.

MIDI merge. To combine two or more MIDI data streams into one.

MIDI mode. A setting on a MIDI device that allows it to respond to incoming messages in a specific way. The primary modes are: Omni On/Poly; Omni On/Mono; Omni Off/Poly; Omni Off/Mono; Multi Mode; Mono Mode.

MIDI time code. A time stamp, similar to SMPTE, that allows MIDI devices to be synchronized with one another.

mids. Abbr. for the frequencies in the middle audible range; i.e, about 200 Hz to 5,000 Hz.

Mingus the Cat. Berklee College of Music's mascot, named after famed jazz bassist and composer Charles Mingus.

miniature score. See study score.

MiniDisc. A digital disc storage device that was manufactured between 1992 and 2013.

minim [Br.]. Half note.

minimalism. A mid- to late-twentieth century musical style that incorporates elements such as a steady pulse, short repetitive figures, slow development of motives, and simple harmonies. Also known as the "New York Hypnotic School."

Minimoog. A groundbreaking commercially available monophonic analog synthesizer invented by electronic music pioneer Robert Moog in 1970.

minor. Pertaining to the minor scale, minor chord, minor key, or minor triad.

minor 7♭5. A seventh chord constructed a minor third, a diminished fifth, and a minor seventh above a root. It is a diatonic seventh chord built on the seventh degree of a major scale and the second degree of a natural minor scale. Also known as a "half-diminished seventh chord" in traditional harmony.

minor chord. A chord whose lowest three notes form a minor triad.

minor key. A tonal area whose primary notes and chords are from a minor scale.

minor pentatonic scale. See Scales in the Appendix.

minor scale. A seven-note scale with the root, 3, and 5 forming a minor triad. The other pitches identify the quality of the minor scale. See Scales in the Appendix.

minor-third half-step scale. See Scales in the Appendix.

minor triad. A three-note chord with a minor third and perfect fifth above the root.

minstrel. (1) An itinerant Medieval singer, musician, and poet. (2) A member of a minstrel show troupe.

minstrel show. An American variety show, popular in the mid-nineteenth century, featuring white actors in blackface performing music, dances, and variety skits.

minuet. A seventeenth-century French country dance in 3/4 meter.

minuet form. See rounded binary.

mirror. (1) A melody and its inversion occurring simultaneously. (2) An entire section or composition played in retrograde following completion of the original.

mirror canon. A canon in retrograde inversion constructed so that the music will sound the same if the performer flips the page upside down. Also known as a "table canon."

mit [Ger.]. With.

mix. (1) To combine multiple audio streams into a mono, stereo, quadraphonic, or other format. (2) The final product of a mixdown.

mixdown. An audio recording process that combines multiple audio streams into a mono, stereo, quadraphonic, or other final mix in which relative levels are set and signal processing may be added.

mixed cadence. In traditional harmony, the extended perfect authentic formula IV V I or IV I6/4 V I.

mixed-media composition. A genre of multimedia artwork in which the elements cannot stand on their own but are dependent on one another, often in a cause and effect relationship.

mixed meter. With more than one meter in close proximity in a song or composition.

mixed orchestration. An arrangement or orchestration that can include a rhythm section, synths, and other nonorchestral instruments along with traditional orchestral instruments.

mixer. An electronic or digital device for routing, combining, and processing audio.

mixing console. An audio recording desk with many channels for routing, processing, and combining sounds.

mixing desk. See mixing console.

Mixolydian ♯4 scale. See also Lydian ♭7 scale. See Scales in the Appendix.

Mixolydian augmented scale. See Scales in the Appendix.

Mixolydian mode. (1) One of the church modes. (2) The chord scale for the V7 chord in a major key. See Scales in the Appendix.

mix stage. See dub stage.

mixture. A stop on a pipe organ that sounds multiple ranks of pipes.

Mlts. Abbr. for mallets.

M.M. Abbr. for metronome marking.

mocker. What John Lennon called himself when he was asked if he was a mod or a rocker.

modal. Music that is organized around one of the modes (Dorian, Phrygian, Lydian, Mixolydian, Aeolian, Locrian).

mode. (1) One of the church modes (Ionian, Dorian, Phrygian, Lydian, Mixolydian, Aeolian). (2) A sequential reordering of a scale; e.g., beginning a harmonic minor scale on the fifth degree.

moderato [It.]. To be played at a medium speed.

modes of limited transposition. Scales that, when transposed, will have fewer than twelve unique sets of pitches, unlike a major scale and its modes.

mods. A British youth subculture from the 1960s that focused on unaggressive pop music and fashion. Their counterparts were the rockers.

modular. A system that is made up of multiple components.

modular synth. A synthesizer developed in the 1950s consisting of separate sections (modules) that are connected by patch cords to create complex systems.

modulation. (1) Moving from one key to another.
(2) Continuous control of any aspect of a sound or signal.

modulation wheel. On a MIDI keyboard, a wheel-shaped continuous controller that controls timbre and expression of a sound.

module. A component of an audio or MIDI system.

mod wheel. Abbr. for modulation wheel.

moll [Ger.]. Minor.

molto [It.]. Very.

Mongolian throat singing. See Tuvan throat singing.

monitor. (1) A loudspeaker or ear device used to listen to the playback of tracks or for performers to hear what they are playing or singing in a live performance. (2) A computer video screen.

mono. Music or sound mixed to a single channel.

monochord. A single-stringed instrument.

monody. (1) Music with only one line. (2) A seventeenth-century Italian recitative-like song.

monophonic. (1) Having only one musical line. (2) An audio recording mixed to a single channel.

monophony. Having a single unaccompanied musical line.

monotone. (1) Played or sung on a single pitch. (2) Chanted on a single pitch.

montage. Overlapping of visual images or musical sounds.

montuno. A syncopated, repeated, ostinato piano vamp in Cuban and Latin music. Also known as a "guajeo."

MOR. Middle of the road, a commercial radio format featuring easy listening music.

mordent. A melodic ornament in which the primary note is embellished by the note underneath it.

morendo [It.]. Dying away.

morris dance. An English stepping-style folk dance performed primarily by men.

mosso [It.]. Quickly, with motion.

motet. A polyphonic choral composition, usually without instrumental accompaniment.

motif. A short melodic fragment that is often used as the basis for a composition. Also called a "motive."

motion. The direction of a music line.

motive. See motif.

moto [It.]. Motion.

Motown. An American popular music style that originated with Motown Records in Detroit in the late 1950s and combined rhythm and blues with pop music.

mountain music. A style of hillbilly roots music originating in the Appalachian mountains of North America.

mouth harp. See jaw harp.

moveable Do. A solfège system in which Do (tonic) can be assigned to any of the twelve chromatic pitches.

movement. A complete section of a larger composition such as a symphony or sonata.

Moviola. A machine for film editing invented in the 1920s, which enables the operator to see and edit a film without using a projector and screen.

MP&E. Music Production and Engineering, one of the departments and majors in the Professional Writing and Technology Division at Berklee College of Music.

MP3. A consumer-level compressed digital audio file format.

MP4. A consumer-level compressed video and digital audio file format.

m.s. Abbr. for mano sinistra.

MTC. Abbr. for MIDI time code.

multimeasure rest. A notational marking indicating that a player is not to play for a prescribed number of measures.

multimedia. A work that employs two or more separate art forms, such as music and video or video and dance.

multineck. A guitar with two or more fretboard necks. See also double neck.

multiphonic. (1) Having many sounds in polyphony. (2) Several notes produced at once on a monophonic instrument.

multitimbral. The capacity for a synthesizer or MIDI device to play multiple sounds at the same time.

multitonic system. A system that employs more than one tonic simultaneously. This concept was put forth by composer and theorist Joseph Schillinger and used by John Coltrane in composing and improvising on "Giant Steps."

multitrack. A recording device, tape or digital, on which more than one track of audio can be recorded and played back.

multivoice improvisation. Improvising more than one line simultaneously.

music. Framed sound.

musica falsa [It.]. See musica ficta.

musica ficta [It.]. (1) Pitch alterations in Medieval music that were not notated but were necessary for performers to stay within the style of the time. (2) Notes outside of the gamut of Medieval music.

musical. See musical theater.

musical saw. A handsaw that is bowed to create a singing, theremin-like sound. Also called a "singing saw."

musical theater. A stage production that features songs, dance, and musical accompaniment, in which, in contrast to opera, the musical selections are interspersed with dialog to move the plot forward.

music artist. An accomplished instrumentalist or singer. Also referred to simply as the "artist."

music bed. Underscore music in a television commercial or other media form that does not include vocals.

music box. An automated musical device developed in the nineteenth century, featuring a mechanism that makes pins pluck metal tines on a rotating cylinder to create repeating simple melodies and accompaniments.

music business. The commercial aspects of music including artist representation, contracts, royalties, promotion, and the like.

music director. (1) A person who organizes and leads a musical ensemble. (2) A music head of a radio station or broadcasting organization. (3) A rehearsal pianist and/or conductor of a musical theater production. (4) A person who supervises musical aspects of a film, television show, advertisement, or video game. Also called a "music supervisor."

music library. (1) A collection of musical scores and books. (2) A collection of copyrighted music in various styles that is licensed for use in film, television, video games, radio, and other media. Also known as a "production music library." See also library music.

musicology. (1) The scholarly study of music. (2) The study of music history, culture, philosophy, and aesthetics. See also historical musicology.

music supervisor. (1) A person who supervises all musical aspects of a film, television show, advertisement, or video game. (2) A person who manages a group of music directors in a musical theater production.

music synchronization. The process of aligning music to visual media.

music synchronization license. An agreement that allows a person or entity to synchronize music to visual media.

music therapy. The use of music in a therapeutic setting to address physical, emotional, cognitive, and social needs of individuals.

musique concrète. A form of tape-recorded music, originating in mid-twentieth-century France, that uses recorded natural sounds, often electronically enhanced, to create musical compositions.

mute. (1) A device that quiets, and often specifically alters, the sound of an acoustic instrument. (2) To silence a recorded track.

muyu. A set of hollow wood fish-shaped blocks that are struck with a wooden stick.

Muzak. A generic term for elevator music, originally produced and sold by the company Muzak Holdings LLC.

nai. Romanian panpipes.

NAMM. National Association of Music Merchants, which puts on trade shows known by the same name.

NARAS. National Academy of Recording Arts and Sciences, the organization that bestows the Grammy awards.

Nashville numbers chart. A music lead sheet using the Nashville number system.

Nashville number system. A shorthand chord and rudimentary rhythm notation system, developed in Nashville recording studios, in which each chord in a diatonic setting is indicated by a number.

Nashville tuning. A tuning system in which the lower four strings on a guitar are tuned up an octave while retaining the normal pitch of the top two, thus giving a bright sound like that of a twelve-string guitar.

native. Software that will run on a computer without additional hardware or supporting software.

natural. A notation symbol cancelling a flat or sharp.

naturale [It.]. Natural.

natural harmonic. An overtone that is part of the naturally occurring harmonic series of a string or resonator.

natural minor scale. A diatonic minor scale with no alterations, constructed W, H, W, W, H, W. It sounds the same as the Aeolian mode. See Scales in the Appendix.

N.C. Abbr. for no chord.

Neapolitan. A major chord or harmony built on the lowered second degree of a scale.

Neapolitan major scale. See Scales in the Appendix.

Neapolitan mandoline. A string instrument with four courses of double strings; an early predecessor of the mandolin in what became the modern tuning of G2, D3, A4, E4.

Neapolitan minor scale. See Scales in the Appendix.

Neapolitan sixth chord. A major triad, in first inversion, built on the lowered second degree of a scale.

near-field monitor. A studio monitor speaker that is designed for close-proximity listening.

neck. The part of a stringed instrument that holds the fingerboard.

neighbor tone. A nonchord tone that moves by half or whole step up or down from the chord tone and then returns to the chord tone.

neobaroque. Music that exhibits the forms and characteristics of Baroque period music but features modern harmonies and musical thinking.

neo bop. A jazz style from the 1980s that emphasized older forms and techniques of jazz as a reaction to free jazz and fusion.

neoclassical. An early twentieth-century style that utilizes the forms and characteristics of Classical period music but features modern harmonies and musical thinking.

neofolk. A late twentieth-century music style, inspired by earlier acoustic folk music and played on both acoustic and electric instruments..

neoromantic. A mid to late twentieth-century style that utilizes the forms and characteristics of Romantic period music but features modern harmonies and musical thinking.

neo-soul. A late twentieth- and early twenty-first century music that emulates and is inspired by 1960s soul music.

neumes. Medieval European notational symbols.

neuro. See neurofunk.

neurofunk. A drum and bass subgenre featuring elements of techstep blended with jazz and funk.

New Age. A style of music popularized in the 1960s that features relaxed, peaceful, slow-moving rhythms along with highly consonant and often static harmonies.

New Age fingerstyle. A style of guitar playing that features gently flowing arpeggios and subdued flamenco-inspired techniques.

newgrass. A form of progressive bluegrass music that incorporates electric instruments, songs from other genres, more adventurous chord progressions, and sometimes lengthy improvisation.

new new wave. See electroclash.

new wave. A stylistically broad pop/rock music genre from the 1980s that was first synonymous with punk but later embraced much of the new pop/rock music of the time.

New York Hypnotic School. See minimalism.

Ni. The Indian solfège syllable for the seventh note of a scale.

nicht [Ger.]. Not.

niente [It.]. Nothing.

ninth. A chord tone that is the interval of a ninth above the root.

nipple gong. A pitched gong named for the nipple-like protrusion at its center.

nocturne. A composition inspired by, or to be performed at, night.

node. (1) A point in a standing wave where there is zero amplitude. (2) A point on a vibrating string that when lightly touched will sound a natural harmonic.

nodes. A condition caused by the growth of nodules on the vocal cords that may result in hoarseness, pain, and restriction of vocal range.

noise shaping. A digital audio technique that increases the apparent signal-to-noise ratio of a signal by moving perceptible noise into masked frequency ranges away from ear-range frequencies.

non [It.]. Not.

nondestructive recording. A digital recording option in which all recorded files are retained.

nonet. An ensemble or composition for nine instruments.

nonharmonic tone. (1) In contemporary harmony, a note that is not a member of a chord. (2) In common-practice harmony, a tone that is not a member of a functional triad. Harmonic sevenths were treated as nonharmonic tones that required a specific resolution.

nonresolving dominant. In tonal harmony, a dominant chord that does not move to any of its typical resolution chords.

nonretrogradable rhythms. Rhythms that sound the same played forward and backward.

non troppo [It.]. Not too much.

noodle. (1) To improvise casually in the background. (2) To warm up by playing small bits of unrelated music.

normalize. To increase an audio file's loudness so its peak is at maximum level without distortion.

Northumbrian pipes. Small bagpipes originating from the English county of Northumbria.

nota cambiata [It.]. See cambiata.

notation. The graphic representation of music.

note. (1) A single musical tone. (2) The graphic representation of a single musical tone.

notehead. In music notation, a graphic representation of a note, commonly elliptical, showing duration, but also found in other shapes, such as a diamond or an x, to specify other timbres or performance techniques.

noveau disco. See electroclash.

nuba. Moroccan classical music suite.

number. A musical selection.

nut. A piece of wood or composite material that holds the strings of a stringed instrument off the fingerboard and apart at the scroll or tuning end of the neck.

nyckelharpa. Swedish fiddle played with keys.

Nyl. Gtr. Abbr. for nylon string guitar.

nylon string guitar. See classical guitar.

Nyquist frequency. Also called the Nyquist limit, it is the highest frequency (half of the sample rate) that can be coded at a given sampling rate in order for a signal to be fully reconstructed.

Ob. Abbr. for oboe.

obbligato [It.]. (1) Necessary, required part. (2) An optional, often highly embellished part.

oblique motion. Melodic movement between two voices in which one voice holds steady as the other moves either up or down.

oboe. (1) A double-reed wind instrument with a range from B♭3 to G6. (2) A member of the oboe double-reed family.

oboe d'amore [It.]. The mezzo-soprano member of the oboe family that has a range from A♭3 to E♭6.

oboe de caccia [It.]. Hunting oboe. A member of the oboe family, it is a transposing instrument in the key of F with a range from F3 to G5.

ocarina. A vessel flute of ancient origins, often made from clay, with four to twelve finger holes and a projecting mouthpiece.

ocean harp. See waterphone.

octatonic scale. An eight-note scale that is constructed by alternating half and whole steps. Also called a "diminished scale" or "whole-half scale." See Scales in the Appendix.

octave. (1) In tempered tuning, a pitch twelve half steps higher or lower than the starting pitch, consequently having the same note name (pitch class). (2) The interval between two notes either double or one half of the first note's frequency.

octavo. A term for a folded sheet music booklet cut in the standard octavo size (7 inches by 10 3/4 inches) and containing a single choral work.

octet. An ensemble or composition for eight players.

odd meter. Any meter that combines simple duple and triple meters.

odd time. Music with an odd meter.

offbeat. (1) A weak beat. (2) A syncopation.

offen [Ger.]. Open.

ohne [Ger.]. Without.

old-time music. A style of acoustic North American folk music, sung and played on fiddles, guitars, and banjos, with roots in Irish, British, and European music.

omni. See omnidirectional or omni mode.

omnidirectional. (1) A microphone that can capture sound equally from all directions. (2) Loudspeakers that project sound equally in all directions.

omni mode. (1) The MIDI setting (mode) in which a MIDI device can receive messages from all channels. (2) MIDI mode setting 1: Omni On/Poly, the setting (mode) in which a MIDI device responds to MIDI data from all channels and is polyphonic.

OMS. Open MIDI System, developed by Opcode Music, Inc., to connect and manage MIDI devices for Macintosh computers.

Ondes Martenot. An early electronic instrument invented in 1928 by French cellist and inventor Maurice Martenot. Uses oscillating vacuum tubes to create a signature eerie, wavering sound.

on top (of the beat). To play precisely with the ictus of a beat or slightly ahead of it, creating a forward push.

open chord. A chord played in open position. Also known as a "cowboy chord."

open harmony. A chord voicing in which there are chord-tone gaps between chord tones.

open position. Chords or melodies played on a guitar or other string instrument in the first position that utilizes open (unstopped) strings.

open string. An unstopped string on a string instrument.

open tuning. Tuning a guitar to a major or minor chord rather than its typical tuning. See also scordatura.

opera. A dramatic musical stage work in which all of the text is sung, thus differentiating it from musical theater.

operetta. A light form of opera.

ophicliede. A keyed brass wind instrument with a range from C2 to C5.

opposite motion. See contrary motion.

opus [It.]. Work, composition.

oratorio. A large-scale sacred music composition for solo singers, choir, and instrumental accompaniment, typically performed without costumes or stage movement.

orchestra. (1) A large group of instruments often in sections by instrument type and family. (2) A large instrumental ensemble with woodwind, brass, percussion, and string sections.

orchestrator. A musician who arranges a musical sketch or existing composition for orchestra.

ordinaire [Fr.]. Ordinary.

Orff instruments. Pitched percussion instruments, modifiable for incremental levels of difficulty, used for elementary music education.

Orff Schulwerk. A music pedagogy created by Gunild Keetman for children based on the ideas of Carl Orff. The innovative approach includes improvisation, movement, singing, and playing.

Org. Abbr. for organ.

organ. (1) A keyboard instrument with a set of pipes of varying sizes through which pressurized air is forced when keys are depressed to sound pitches. Also known as a pipe organ. (2) An electronic or digital version of a pipe organ in which the sounds of the pipes are electronically reproduced or synthesized. (3) A forced-air instrument that utilizes bellows or blowing to sound a bank of reeds.

organ stop. A knob on a pipe organ that, when pulled, allows pressurized air to pass through a pipe or multiple pipes, creating a specific pitch and timbre.

organum. Medieval plainchant in which at least one other voice is added to the primary melody to enrich the harmony.

Oriental scale. See Scales in the Appendix.

ornament. A melodic embellishment.

Oscar. An award given by the Academy of Motion Picture Arts and Sciences.

oscillator. A digital or electronic device that creates a repeating signal, most often a sine wave, of a specific frequency.

ossia [It.]. An alternate part.

ostinato [It.]. A repeating part or figure.

ottavo [It.]. Octave.

oud. An unfretted, plucked string instrument of southern Mesopotamian origin that is the ancestor of the lute and guitar. It is pear-shaped and most often has five courses of high strings and a single lower string.

outer form. The overarching frame of a song or extended composition, which may include any number of subsections.

out head. The closing melody of a jazz tune after solos have been taken.

out playing. Free improvisation usually without a clear form, tonal center, or harmony.

output signal. The signal that comes out of an electronic system.

outro. The concluding section of a song or piece of music.

ouvert [Fr.]. Open.

ovation. A positive and large audience response to a performance.

overblow. To blow forcefully across an edge-blown wind instrument's mouthpiece causing the higher overtones to dominate the resulting sound.

overdrive. Distortion of an electrical signal as gain is increased.

overdub. To record over a previously recorded track.

overture. (1) The musical introduction to a larger work such as an opera, oratorio, or musical. (2) A freestanding programmatic piece of music. See also French overture.

p. Abbr. for piano (softly).

Pa. The Indian solfège syllable for the fifth note of a scale.

PA. Public address system, a sound reinforcement system for amplifying voices and musical instruments.

pad. (1) A sustained chord or texture. (2) A circuit designed to attenuate an electronic device's output signal.

pagode. Brazilian samba style.

palm mute. Using the palm of the nonfretting hand to mute a guitar, bass, banjo, mandolin, or other stringed instrument.

palm-wine music. West African party music.

pan. To position a sound at a certain point in a stereo, quadraphonic, or other multiple speaker field.

panchromatic. Using all of the twelve pitches.

Pandean pipes. See panpipes.

pandeiro. Brazilian hand frame drum.

pandiatonic. Exclusively using the notes of a scale without any one acting as tonic.

pandura. An ancient Greek three-stringed plucked instrument.

pan flute. See panpipes.

panpipes. An edge-blown wind instrument constructed from a set of graduated length pipes that are fastened together.

pans. Steel drums.

pantonal. Including all tonalities.

paradiddle. A drum rudiment consisting of a series of sixteenth notes grouped in fours or sixes with alternating patterns such as RLRR LRLL.

paradinhas. Rhythm breaks performed by the bateria in Brazilian samba.

parallelism. The parallel melodic or chord movement of two or more parts. See also planing.

parallel-key modulation. A change of key (modulation) in which the tonic of each key is the same, e.g., C major to C minor.

parallel motion. Melodic movement between two or more voices in which the voices move in the same direction simultaneously.

parallel period. A musical period in which the two phrases are very similar, except that the second ends in a perfect authentic cadence.

parameter. Any controllable element of sound.

parametric EQ. An audio equalizer that has multiple bands throughout the audible frequency spectrum. These can be individually adjusted for center frequency, bandwidth, and amplitude.

parlando [It.]. As if spoken.

parlante [It.]. See parlando.

partial. The fundamental and individual overtones of a complex wave.

partita. (1) An eighteenth-century suite for a solo instrument. (2) A set of instrumental variations.

part singing. When two or more performers sing different, yet harmonious, lines.

part song. A song, often unaccompanied, with two or more separate harmonious melodic lines sung by the performers.

paso doble. (1) A lively Spanish dance in 2/4 meter. (2) A march played at a bullfight.

passacaglia. (1) A slow Spanish dance in triple meter. (2) A set of continuous variations over a repeating harmonic structure.

passage. (1) A complete musical thought that often connects two sections of music. (2) A moving scalar melodic line, often in a concerto, that develops a musical motif.

passing tone. A nonharmonic tone that moves in stepwise motion and connects two chord tones.

patch. (1) A specific configuration of synthesizer modules made with patch cords. (2) Configurations and software connections kept in a computer's or musical device's memory.

patch bay. A hardware hub in which various musical devices and peripherals can be connected.

patch cord. An electric cable for connecting instruments, amplifiers, and musical devices.

patter song. A song in a fast, rhythmic style, which mimics speech patterns and is often humorous.

patter talk. A fast, rhythmic style of nonpitched, but contoured, singing that mimics speech patterns. See also Sprechstimme.

pavane. A slow, regal, processional dance performed in sixteenth- and seventeenth-century Europe.

pavillions en l'air [Fr.]. Bells of brass instrument(s) held high.

payola. The illegal payment of cash or gifts by record companies to radio stations in exchange for airplay.

PCM. Abbr. for pulse code modulation.

peak. The highest point of a waveform or audio signal.

Peak. A digital audio editing software program.

ped. Abbr. for pedal.

pedal. (1) A sustained note under or over moving lines or harmonies. (2) A stompbox or other foot-controlled effects processor. (3) In piano music, an indication to press one of the three foot pedals. (4) Short for "pedal tone."

pedal board. A board onto which foot-controlled effects processors are mounted.

pedal marks. Indications in notated music for the player to depress or release one of the pedals, typically the sustain pedal if there is no other pedal specified.

pedal point. A held note under or over moving lines or harmonies.

pedal steel guitar. A guitar-like instrument mounted horizontally on a frame and played with a sliding steel bar rather than fingers. The instrument has tuning rods to facilitate rapid changes in tuning as well as knee-operated pitch-changing levers.

pedal tone. (1) The lowest possible note (fundamental) in a harmonic series of a cylindrical-bore brass instrument. (2) See pedal point.

peg. A moveable tapered cylindrical wooden dowel inserted into the head of a string instrument, connected to a string, and turned to tighten or loosen the string for tuning.

pelog scale. One of the two primary Indonesian scales. See Scales in the Appendix.

penny whistle. A six-holed, end-blown fipple flute originating in the British Isles. Also known as a "tin whistle" and an "Irish whistle."

pentachord. A set of five notes.

pentad. A five-note chord.

pentatonic scale. A five-note scale.

pep band. An ensemble that plays at sporting events and other gatherings with the purpose of exciting the crowd.

pep section. (1)The Duke Ellington Orchestra's three-man trombone section. (2) Subsequently, a trio of any three brass instruments featured in a big band arrangement.

percussion. (1) Instruments that are struck or scraped to generate sound. (2) The section of a band, ensemble, or orchestra that includes drums, cymbals, and other percussion instruments.

perfect authentic cadence. A harmonic cadence that ends V I, with both ending chords in root position and with the tonic in the soprano of the final chord.

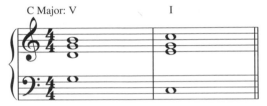

perfect fifth. In Western music, a musical interval with a 3:2 ratio that consists of seven half steps.

perfect fourth. In Western music, a musical interval with a 4:3 ratio that consists of five half steps.

perfect intervals. The unison, fourth, fifth, and octave.

perfect octave. In Western music, a musical interval with a 2:1 ratio that consists of twelve half steps.

perfect pitch. The ability to recognize any note played on an instrument or sung.

perfect unison. In Western music, a musical interval with a 1:1 ratio that consists of zero steps and is the first note of a major or minor scale.

period. (1) A formal unit in music that consists of two (sometimes more) phrases, typically with the first phrase ending with an inconclusive cadence and the second with a perfect authentic cadence. (2) An era in music history such as the Baroque or Romantic period.

permutation. A reordering of a set of pitches.

perpetual canon. A musical canon that can go on indefinitely by the subject leading back to its own beginning. Also called a "circular canon."

Persian scale. See Scales in the Appendix.

pesante [It.]. Heavy, weighty.

peu [Fr.]. A little.

phantom image. The optimal stereo image that is heard when listening to two speakers.

phantom power. Electrical voltage carried through an XLR connector which sends power to a microphone transducer with active electronics.

phase. A particular point in the cycle of a waveform, measured as an angle in degrees.

phase cancellation. Silence that is the result of two sound waves of the same frequency being 180 degrees out of phase with one another.

phase music. A genre associated with minimalist music due to its technique of multiple repetitions. Phasing occurs when motives or recorded sound from two or more sources are repeated and become gradually unaligned.

phase shifter. An effects device that changes the phase of a signal by slightly delaying it and then mixing it with the original signal, creating an undulating sound.

phat. (1) Excellent. (2) A sound that has a pleasing loudness and punch.

Philly sound. A style of soul music associated with Philadelphia in the 1960s and 1970s, which featured horns and lush strings.

phone plug. An analog audio connector originally developed for telephones, now used for audio connections, such as guitar to amplifier.

phono plug. A coaxial audio connector that was developed to connect components of a phonograph system.

phrase. A formal melodic, harmonic, or rhythmic unit in music that is a complete musical thought akin to a written sentence.

phrase mark. See slur.

Phrygian dominant scale. See Scales in the Appendix.

Phrygian half cadence. A harmonic cadence that ends IVmi V with the IVmi chord in the first inversion.

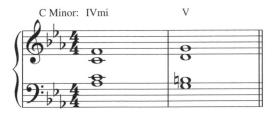

Phrygian minor scale. See Phrygian mode.

Phrygian mode. (1) A Medieval church mode that can be represented by the white keys of a piano spanning E to E. (2) A modal minor scale constructed H, W, W, W, H, W, W. (3) A chord scale from the IIImi7 of a major key. See Scales in the Appendix.

pianica. See melodica.

pianissimo [It.]. Very softly.

pianississimo [It.]. Very, very softly.

piano [It.]. (1) Soft. (2) A keyboard instrument in which hammers strike strings when depressed.

piano bar. A lounge or bar that has a piano player as the primary entertainer.

pianoforte. See piano.

piano reduction. A score of a larger ensemble composition that has been stripped down to its essential elements so it can be played on a piano. Also called a "reduced score."

piano trio. An ensemble with piano, violin, and cello.

piatti [It.]. Cymbals.

Picardy third. Ending a minor key composition with a cadence of V to I major instead of the expected I minor chord.

Picc. Abbr. for piccolo.

piccolo. A woodwind instrument of the flute family. It is half the size of the standard flute and has a range of C5 to C8.

pick. (1) A small, flat, heart-shaped implement that is made from plastic, wood, metal, or other solid material that is used to pluck the strings of a guitar or other stringed instrument. Also called a "plectrum." (2) To pluck a stringed instrument.

pick guard. A plate on a guitar or other stringed instrument that is designed to protect the face of the instrument from damage from picking.

pick scrape. A guitar technique in which the edge of a pick is dragged lengthwise across a string to create a gritty sound.

pickup. (1) Unaccented note preceding a strong beat; upbeat. (2) The electric coil transducer on an electric guitar, bass, or other stringed instrument. (3) A point in a film score where music is to be inserted (punched in).

pickup notes. Notes preceding, and leading to, the first bar of a song or other musical composition.

picture lock. See locked picture.

piece. A musical composition.

Piedmont blues. A southeastern U.S. blues style that features fingerpicked acoustic guitar with the thumb playing a syncopated bass rhythm and the melody picked on the high strings. It is an upbeat music influenced by ragtime.

pieno [It.]. Full.

piezo. Short for piezoelectric.

piezoelectric. Instrument pickups, especially popular for stringed instruments, that transform the instrument's vibrations into an electrical signal, which is then amplified and broadcast.

pink noise. Sound energy (random noise) distributed uniformly by octave throughout the audio spectrum. Also referred to as "1/f noise" or "flicker noise."

pipe organ. See organ.

piston. A valve in a trumpet or other valved brass instrument.

pitch. (1) An individual musical note. (2) A specific sound-wave frequency. (3) Shortening of perfect pitch.

pitch bend. (1) A MIDI control message sent by a wheel or lever for a note to be raised or lowered incrementally. (2) The incremental raising or lowering of a note achieved by stretching a string, squeezing a reed, or lipping.

pitch class. A note and all of its octave transpositions.

pitch-class set. An unordered group of unique pitches, not including duplicates and octave equivalents.

pitch correction. The retuning of notes on a recording, a track, or in real time to conform with a desired tuning system.

pitch pipe. A device that, when blown into, produces a specific note or notes to aid in tuning an instrument or voices.

pitch shifter. A device or algorithm that moves a given note up or down in designated increments.

pit orchestra. An ensemble that plays for musicals, theater productions, and other stage productions. So called due to the ensemble being placed in a space below the level of the stage and therefore out of direct audience view.

piu [It.]. More.

piu mosso [It.]. More motion (faster).

pivot chord. A chord used for modulation that functions in both the current key and the target key and creates a smooth transition.

pivot modulation. A modulation utilizing a pivot chord. See pivot chord.

pizzicato [It.]. Plucked.

plagal cadence. A harmonic cadence that ends IV I.

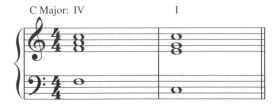

plainchant. Monophonic liturgical chant of the early Roman Catholic Church. See also Gregorian chant.

plainsong. See plainchant.

planing. Parallel motion of a series of intervals or chords.

plate reverb. An early reverb system used in recording in which a metal plate is vibrated with a transducer. The "reverberated" result is then captured by a contact microphone and mixed into the overall sound.

platinum record. A certification that an album or single has sold at least one million units.

player piano. An automated mechanical piano that uses preprogrammed perforated music rolls to play songs and compositions.

playing inside. Jazz improvising following the changes and using the most normal chord scales.

playing outside. Jazz improvising not following the changes. Often using atonal materials.

playlist. (1) In hard-disk recording, a list of audio that can be played in a specified order. (2) A radio station's list of the songs that are put into play rotation. (3) On a computer or other device, a list of songs that a user can play in the order he or she desires.

plectrum. See pick.

plop. A brass or wind effect in which the player starts from an indefinite pitch, quickly plays down a scale, and ends on the target note. The plop is typically preceded by a rest.

plosive. A consonant, such as a "p" or "b," sung or spoken with a sudden burst of air.

plug and play. A device or musical instrument that can be directly connected with a computer and work without drivers or other additional software.

plug-in. A software component (often, for signal processing) that can be accessed from within a larger software application, such as a DAW or notation program.

plunger mute. A brass instrument mute that is either actually the cup of a sink plunger or resembles one.

plus [Fr.]. More.

Pno. Abbr. for piano.

PnP. Abbr. for plug and play.

pocket. (1) The center of a beat, not ahead or behind it. (2) Played precisely in that fashion; i.e., in the pocket.

poco [It.]. Little.

poco a poco [It.]. Little by little.

podcast. An audio program that is distributed in a digital format, often online. Originally made to be played on an iPod but is no longer device specific.

pogo. Punk-era dance in which the dancer jumps straight up and down.

polar pattern. A plot or graph showing the pattern in which a microphone picks up sound coming from a sound source.

polka. A bouncy and upbeat dance in 2/4 meter originating from Bohemia.

polonaise. A Polish gliding dance in 3/4 meter.

polska. A Swedish dance in triple meter.

polychord. (1) A chord constructed from two or more separate chords (usually triads) stacked over one another. (2) An instrument with many strings.

polymeter. A rhythmic device, in which the music maintains a common beat, yet is in two or more meters simultaneously; e.g., four bars of 5/4 sounding as five bars of 4/4.

polyphony. (1) Two or more melodies with independent rhythms sounding simultaneously. (2) The number of notes a MIDI or other audio device can play simultaneously.

polyrhythm. Simultaneous combination of contrasting rhythms.

polytonality. The use of two or more different keys at the same time.

pomo. Short for postmodern.

ponticello [It.]. Bowed on or near the bridge.

pop. A music genre of short songs that often feature simple harmonies, strong catchy melodies and lyrics, clear beats, and repeated choruses.

pop ballad. See rock ballad.

pop filter. A microphone screen designed to eliminate or reduce sudden audible bursts of air created by vocal plosives such as "p" or "b."

pops. An orchestra that plays light classical and popular tunes.

porch. A laid-back tempo, feel, and style, as though on the porch of a house.

port. (1) An input, such as for MIDI or SCSI, that connects external devices and instruments. (2) An opening in a speaker enclosure that is fine-tuned to provide the best acoustical response.

portamento [It.]. A short glide or slide into a pitch. See also glissando.

portato [It.]. A bow stroke between legato and staccato.

Posaune [Ger.]. Trombone.

position. A specific hand placement when playing a string instrument, trombone, and others; e.g., the placement of the fretting hand on the first five frets closest to the head of a guitar is called "first position."

post-bop. A subgenre of jazz music that evolved in the early 1960s featuring small combos, freer forms, tempos, and meters; and music composed by the performers.

postlude. (1) An organ piece, usually improvised, played at the end of a church service. (2) A coda.

postmodern. Starting in the 1960s, a broad descriptor of music, both popular and classical, that exhibits a blending of high and low styles and does not adhere to any one school of composition or thought.

postproduction. After the initial recording of tracks or film is completed, the stage at which editing, adding effects, mixing, mastering, and other procedures are done.

pot. Abbr. for potentiometer.

potentiometer. A knob that controls the output of a system.

power ballad. A slow-tempo song in a rock or pop style, which often features a highly orchestrated emotional chorus.

power chord. A chord that is much used in rock and heavy metal music of the 1980s and beyond, and consists of a root and a perfect fifth or a root and a perfect fourth, both often doubling the root at the octave.

powered monitor. A monitor loudspeaker that has its own power source and does not require an external amplifier.

powered speaker. A loudspeaker that has its own power source and does not require an external amplifier.

power pop. A music genre that emerged in the 1980s and draws its sound and inspiration from the melodic, focused popular music of the 1960s. The music features hooky vocals and electric guitar riffs, sparse arrangements, and no, or only limited, solos.

pp. Abbr. for pianissimo.

ppp. Abbr. for pianississimo.

PPQ. Abbr. for pulses per quarter note. Used in MIDI protocol.

preamp. Short for preamplifier.

preamplifier. An amplifier that boosts a weak signal, such as one from a microphone, to a useable level while introducing the smallest amount of noise and distortion possible.

prebend. A guitar technique in which a string is bent (stretched upward with the fretting hand) before it is plucked with a pick or finger.

precedence effect. The perception of a single fused sound from two sounds in which the first sound, which is dominant, is followed very closely by a second sound. Also known as the "Haas effect."

prechorus. A transitional section in a song that builds to the chorus.

precomposition. The imaginative, preparatory, drafting stage of composition.

predelay. A reverb processing parameter in which the amount of time between the onset of a dry signal and the first reflections can be set to a user-desired length.

predominant. A chord, such as a German sixth, that normally precedes and resolves to a dominant chord.

prelay. Music recorded by a composer prior to a recording session.

prelude. (1) A section or piece of music that is composed as an introduction to a larger section or piece. (2) A short, independent composition, often for piano.

prepared instrument. A musical instrument whose normal characteristics have been altered to create new sounds; e.g., a guitar in which wax paper is inserted between strings to create a buzzing effect.

prepared piano. A piano whose normal playing characteristics have been altered to create new sounds; e.g., one in which pennies are threaded between the strings to create bell-like tones.

preproduction. Activities, elements, and preparation that precede the start of a project such as a film, a recording, or a performance.

pre-records. Music that is recorded prior to a recording session and is to be played during the session and mixed with the live music.

pres [It.]. Near.

preset. An instrument patch or program that has been created by an electronic instrument or device manufacturer and comes with the product.

press. (1) A publishing company that prints and distributes books and music scores. (2) To make physical copies of CDs and vinyl records.

press kit. Prepackaged promotional materials given to the media and others to showcase a band or an artist.

pressure sensitive. When a MIDI keyboard recognizes the amount of weight applied on a key by the fingers of a player.

prestissimo [It.]. Extremely fast.

presto [It.]. Very fast.

prima donna. (1) The principal female singer in an opera. (2) A stuck-up, self-important musician—either male or female.

prime. The original form of a row in serial music.

print. To record.

process music. A composition in which short musical motives of varying lengths are overlapped. So named because the process is as important as the result.

producer. (1) A person who guides the creative process of a recording project as well as hiring musicians and coordinating all aspects of a session. (2) A person who oversees all aspects of a film's production, such as hiring scriptwriters, cast, and crew; budgeting; and distribution.

production music library. See music library.

production suite. A space with a DAW, and often an iso booth, that is dedicated to creating, recording, mixing, and mastering music.

program music. Music that is composed to aurally tell or describe a story, event, or narrative. Not intended for visual media.

progression. (1) A specified series of chords or harmonies. (2) The forward harmonic movement of a composition propelled by strong root motion. (3) The chords to a song.

progressive jazz. (1) Jazz music that is infused with elements from other genres. (2) Free style and cool jazz music recorded by Progressive Records in the 1950s.

progressive rock. See art rock.

prog rock. See art rock.

prolation canon. See mensuration canon.

prolongation. (1) A note or harmony that is understood to continue sounding although it is no longer present in the actual music. (2) A concept in Schenkerian analysis in which the voice leading moves from one level to the next.

Prometheus scale. A scale used in Russian composer Scriabin's symphonic composition *Prometheus: The Poem of Fire* (1910). See Scales in the Appendix.

promoter. A music industry professional who is paid to bring attention to and to market a band, an artist, or a concert.

proportional notation. Music written (notated) so that time equals horizontal space.

prosody. (1) The rhythms of speech. (2) The study of the structure of poetry and lyrics.

prosumer. A designation for gear that is between consumer and professional level in quality.

Pro Tools. A professional-level digital recording, sequencing, editing, and mixing application (DAW).

protoprogression. The original set of chords (progression) to which substitutions and reharmonizations have been applied.

proximity effect. The increase in low frequency response when a sound source gets closer to a microphone.

PRS. Performing Right Society, a U.K. collecting agent for songwriters, composers, and music publishers.

psalm. Sacred song or hymn.

psalm tone. A simple melody and/or reciting tone used for singing psalms in Gregorian chant. There are eight tones, one for each of the church modes.

psaltery. An ancient, plucked, harp-like string instrument of Greek origin.

psychedelic rock. A subgenre of rock music that attempts to musically describe and/or enhance the mind-altering hallucinogenic experiences that were part of late-1960s culture. See also acid rock.

psychoacoustics. The study of the physical and psychological effects of sound.

PT. Abbr. for Pro Tools.

publisher. (1) A company that licenses music, tracks usage, and collects royalties for a songwriter or composer in exchange for being assigned copyright. (2) A company that prints and sells notated music.

pub rock. A British back-to-basis subgenre of rock music that emerged in the early 1970s in reaction to the more complicated and sophisticated progressive rock of the era.

pull-off. A strings instrument technique in which the fingering hand plucks a string by pulling it off the fingerboard.

pulse. The primary beat in music.

pulse code modulation. A method used to digitally represent analog sound waves by sampling the wave and representing it in digital amplitude graphs.

pulse wave. A waveform that instantaneously moves from negative to positive and vice versa.

pumping. A term used for the sound caused by a large amount of compression or gating being applied to a sound file or recording. Also called "breathing."

pump organ. See harmonium.

punch. A rhythmic accent often coupled with a chord.

punches. A circular flash in a film or video that marks the point of an important hit. Used in conjunction with streamers.

punches and streamers. In film, timing marks consisting of a vertical line followed by a flash. See also punches and streamer.

punch in. To overdub new material on a segment of a previously recorded track to fix or improve the earlier performance.

punk rock. A genre of hard-edged, pared-down rock music, often with antiestablishment lyrics, which emerged in Britain in the 1970s.

purfling. The ornamental edging on the face and sometimes back of a string instrument such as a violin or guitar.

push. A rhythmic anticipation often coupled with a chord.

puzzle canon. See riddle canon.

Pythagorean comma. See comma

quad. See quadraphonic.

quadraphonic. Music that is mixed to four independent channels, most often two front and two back.

quadrille. A French couples' dance with music alternating in 6/8 and 2/4.

quadrivium. The group of the four Medieval mathematical arts: music, number, geometry, and cosmology.

quadruplet. A tuplet with four notes in the time of three.

quantization. (1) In MIDI sequencing, rounding out to the nearest user-specified note value (quarter, eighth, sixteenth, etc.). (2) In digital audio, rounding off to a user-specified portion of time.

quartal. Harmonies built in fourths rather than the more typical thirds.

quarter note. A note with one quarter the value of a whole note.

quarter rest. A rest with one fourth of the value of a whole rest, receiving one beat in 4/4 time.

quarter step. See quarter tone.

quarter tone. An interval half the size of a semitone (half step).

quarter track. An analog tape recorder with a head that records four tracks.

quartet. (1) A composition for four performers. (2) A group of four performers.

quasi. [Lat.]. "Almost," or "almost as if."

quaver [Br.]. Eighth note.

quick change blues. See quick four.

quick four. Moving to the IV chord in the second bar of twelve-bar blues.

QuickTime instruments. Software instruments that come with QuickTime video software.

quintet. (1) A composition for five performers. (2) A group of five performers.

quintuplet. A tuplet with five notes in the space of four.

quitra. A North African instrument with eight strings in four courses.

quodlibet. A composition that uses two or more familiar melodies, often contrapuntally and in a lighthearted manner.

R&B. Rhythm and blues, a popular genre originating in the African American music community in the 1940s and rooted in jazz and blues. Later broadened to include soul and gospel influences.

Ra. The solfège syllable for a lowered second degree of a major or minor scale.

rabab. Middle Eastern bowed string instrument.

rack. A box-shaped case that holds sound modules and other audio gear.

raga. A scale and melodic pattern in Indian music.

raga todi. See Scales in the Appendix.

raga marva. See Scales in the Appendix.

ragga. Aggressive form of dancehall music developed in the mid 1980s.

ragga drum and bass. A drum and bass subgenre featuring influences from reggae and dancehall music.

ragga jungle. A musical style with influences from reggae and dancehall music, featuring jungle breakbeats, rudeboy lyrics, reggae bass lines, and sound clashes.

ragtime. An upbeat and syncopated genre of American music that was popular in the early twentieth century. In 1897, Ben Harney's publication of the *Ragtime Instructor* propelled the music into the national limelight.

rai. Algerian protest music.

railroad tracks. A caesura.

rallentando [It.]. Slowing in tempo.

ramp wave. See sawtooth wave.

range. (1) The distance between the lowest and highest note. (2) The tessitura of a singer's voice.

rap. A genre of music with roots in African American culture, which features rhythmically spoken rhyming verses set to, or implying, a beat. Although it is a unique earlier genre, rap has become closely associated with hip-hop and is often thought of as being synonymous with it.

rasgado [Sp.]. A fast, sweeping strum across the strings of a guitar, which creates an arpeggio-like sound.

rasgueado [Sp.]. See rasgado.

ratamacue. A percussion rudiment that consists of a drag to a triplet followed by a single stroke.

rate. A parameter that sets or describes the speed of modulation of a synthesizer.

rattle. A percussion instrument that is shaken to produce a sound.

Re. (1) The solfège syllable for the second note of a major scale. (2) The note D in fixed Do solfège. (3) The Hindustani Indian solfège syllable for the second note of a scale.

read the ink. In jazz, direction to play exactly what is written in the music.

real answer. A comes (answer) in a fugue that is an intervallicly exact transposed copy of the dux (leader).

Real Book. A lead sheet compilation of jazz tunes and standards.

real sequence. A sequence in which the repetition is an exact transposition of the original motif or phrase.

real time. Immediate action or response as opposed to delayed response.

real-time mode. A mode of operation on a digital device or processor in which the contents of memory, peripheral, and register locations can be modified while the processor is running and executing code.

Reason. A popular MIDI, digital recording, mixing, and editing application by Propellerhead Software.

rebec. A Renaissance-era bowed stringed instrument with one to five strings.

recap. See recapitulation.

recapitulation. (1) The return of the first section of a movement or composition in sonata form. (2) A repeat of the primary section at the end of a composition or movement.

recital. A formal concert of music typically featuring one or two performers.

recitative. Singing that imitates the inflections of spoken words, often in rhythm and tempo.

reciting tone. A note (the fifth degree of the appropriate church mode) on which much of a psalm verse is chanted. See also psalm tone.

recorder. (1) An end-blown fipple flute with seven finger holes. (2) See tape recorder and recording device.

recording console. See mixing console.

recording device. A digital or analog machine for capturing and storing sound and music.

recording engineer. A music professional who is skilled in the equipment and methods for capturing audio. See also audio engineer.

recording studio. A space that is dedicated to capturing, producing, and mixing audio.

recursive loop. See feedback loop.

Red Book. A book of standards for audio compact discs, which includes specifications on organization, audio formats, and physical and optical characteristics.

reduced score. An ensemble score that has been arranged for a smaller number of instruments than it was originally written for or for piano alone.

reduction. See reduced score.

reed. (1) A thin section of cane, metal, or other vibrating material that is attached to an instrument at one end and can be set into motion by a current of air either blown across or forced across it to create a musical tone. (2) An instrument that utilizes a reed for sound production.

reel. (1) A length of motion picture film wrapped around a cylinder. In the early days of cinema, one reel was about ten minutes of movie. (2) A portion of a film ready to be scored. (3) An audiotape. (4) An audio archive. (5) A brisk Irish folk dance in common time.

reel-to-reel. An analog tape recorder that has two reels to spool magnetic recording tape that passes through a recording and playback head.

reen. A really terrible musical performance.

reference mix. See reference track.

reference track. (1) In audio recording, a very good recording (often a commercial release) to use for comparison or emulation when mixing or mastering. (2) A track that is used as a guide in overdubbing.

refrain. (1) A repeated section of a song, usually following a verse, in which the words and melody are similar at each occurrence. (2) A repeated section or title line in a vocal composition. Also called a "chorus."

reggae. A genre of Jamaican music that evolved from ska and rocksteady in the 1960s and features a steady bass line and sixteenth-note guitar syncopations.

reggaeton. A blend of reggae and Latin music originating in Puerto Rico in the 1980s. Also called "Spanish reggae."

register. A portion of the range, or tessitura, of a voice or instrument.

registration. The combination of organ or harpsichord stops used for a piece, or section of a piece, of music.

reharm. Short for reharmonization.

reharmonization. Taking an existing song and substituting the chords with an alternate version.

rehearsal marking. A number or letter connected to specific measures on a score and to all of the instrumental parts, which enables the performers and conductor to easily locate a point in the music.

rehearsal numbers. See rehearsal marking.

relative-key modulation. Changing key (modulating) from a major key to its relative minor or from a minor key to its relative major.

relative major. (1) A major key that has the same key signature as a minor key. (2) A major scale that has the same number of flats and sharps as a minor scale.

relative minor. (1) A minor key that has the same key signature as a major key. (2) A minor scale that has the same number of flats and sharps as a major scale.

relative pitch. After hearing a given note, the ability to identify other notes by letter name.

release. The final segment of an ADSR (attack, decay, sustain, release) envelope generator as used in music synthesis.

remaster. To rebalance the final mix of a recording, often utilizing techniques and equipment that was not available at the time of the original mastering.

rembétika. Urban Greek music style.

remix. To rebalance (mix) the stems of an existing recording, sometimes adding new material and processing. See also mashup.

remote key. A key whose key signature is two or more accidentals removed from the starting key.

Renaissance. A style period in European classical music that roughly spans 1425 to 1600.

repeat. A score marking indicating that a section of music is to be played again.

reprise. To repeat a piece or section of a piece.

requiem. (1) A memorial piece. (2) A mass for the dead in the Roman Catholic Church.

resolution. The movement of a dissonant note or chord to a consonant note or chord.

response. A musical reply to a phrase or section of music.

rest. A notation element indicating that a performer is not to play for the indicated duration.

restatement. See recapitulation.

rest stroke. See apoyando.

resultant tone. See combination tone.

retardation suspension. An upward resolving suspension such as scale degree 7 to scale degree 1.

retro. A musical style or product that has been recreated to emulate or imitate a previous version.

retro electro. See electroclash.

retrograde. A backwards version of a melody or rhythm.

retrogression. Weak chord motion; e.g., V IImi VImi IIImi.

return. (1) The opposite of a send in an audio mixer. (2) The input to return the processed signal set from a send to a device.

reveille. A military bugle call played at sunrise.

reverb. (1) Short for reverberation. (2) A digital or analog device designed to emulate reverberation. Also called a "reverb unit."

reverberation. The number, strength, and decay of sound reflections based on the size and construction of a space.

reverb unit. See reverb.

rewire. In computer and electronic music, making one application or device the slave of another application or device.

rhapsody. A free-form compositional fantasy often with nationalist or epic influences.

Rhodes electric piano. See Fender Rhodes.

rhumba. See rumba.

rhythm. The movement in time of musical impulses often grouped into recurring patterns.

rhythm and blues. See R&B.

rhythm changes. A chord progression from Gershwin's "I Got Rhythm," played in AABA form and used as the basis for many jazz tunes.

rhythm guitar. The guitar part in a band that primarily plays chords.

rhythmic displacement. To repeat a motive or line starting at a different point in a measure.

rhythmic modulation. See metric modulation.

rhythm section. The group of instruments in a band that provides the rhythmic and harmonic support. Typically, drums, bass, guitar, and/or a keyboard instrument.

Ri. (1) The solfège name for the raised second degree of a major scale. (2) The Indian Carnatic solfège syllable for the second note of a scale.

RIAA. Recording Industry Association of America.

ribbon mic. A highly sensitive microphone that captures sound by measuring velocity via a thin strip in a magnetic field.

ricercare. A sixteenth- and seventeenth-century imitative instrumental composition.

Rickenbacker. An electric guitar brought into the international limelight because of its use by George Harrison and John Lennon during the Beatles' heyday.

ricochet. In string playing, a bow stroke in which the bow is dropped on the string and rebounds to create a series of fast staccato notes.

riddle canon. A canon that comes with often obscure clues regarding when and what pitch interval the imitation begins. Also known as a "puzzle canon."

ride cymbal. A suspended cymbal that is part of a drum set and is used for timekeeping and repeating rhythms.

riff. (1) A short, repeated phrase or motif that is played over chord changes, often as a background for a soloist. (2) A musical lick.

rim shot. A loud simultaneous strike with a stick on both the frame and head of a snare drum.

rinforzando [It.]. Reinforced, heavy.

ring modulator. An audio processor that outputs the sum and difference of input frequencies, resulting in a complex and often tinny mechanical sound.

ring shout. An African American musical religious ritual.

rip. A jazz arranging and performance technique in which the player (usually brass or woodwind) executes a rapid upward glissando to an indefinite pitch.

ripieno. The full orchestra in a concerto grosso.

riq. Egyptian percussion instrument similar to a small tambourine.

risoluto [It.]. Resolutely.

rit. [It.]. Abbr. for ritardando.

ritard [It.]. Short for ritardando.

ritardando [It.]. Decreasing in tempo.

ritenuto [It.]. Immediately decreasing in tempo.

RMS. Abbr. for root mean square.

roadie. Someone who hauls, sets up, and breaks down a band's equipment as well as performing other tasks to assist the band.

rock. A broad category of popular music whose name and style has its roots in 1950s rock and roll. Rock groups typically consist of electric guitar, electric bass, drums, keyboards, and vocals.

rock and roll. A popular music style that began in the United States in the 1940s and 1950s, with roots in jump blues, jazz, country, and country swing.

rockabilly. Combination of rock and hillbilly music.

rock ballad. A slow-tempo song often in a strophic folk-rock style.

rockers. A 1960s British youth subculture, associated with motorcycles, leather jackets, and pompadour hairstyles, which favored 1950s rock and roll.

rock opera. A genre of opera that emerged in the 1960s and connects songs through a narrative. The performance is by a rock band in concert, typically without any staging or acting.

rocksteady. A Jamaican music style that emerged in the 1960s combining elements of ska, jazz, R&B, and Latin music.

rockumentary. A documentary about rock or pop musicians and music.

rococo. A highly ornate style of European art music from about 1725 to 1775.

roll. A sustained drum trill created by alternating left and right mallets, sticks, or hands.

rolled chord. An arpeggiated chord on a piano or keyboard instrument.

romance. An instrumental composition that is lyrical in character and is not expected to have a formal structure.

Romanian scale. See Scales in the Appendix.

Romantic. A style of European classical music that flourished from approximately 1825 to 1900.

rondeau. An accompanied Medieval period song featuring alternating arias and refrains.

rondo. A classical music form in which the main theme or section alternates with contrasting material creating forms such as ABABA and ABACABA, etc.

root. The lowest note of a triad or chord in its fundamental position.

root motion. The movement of chord fundamentals (roots).

roots music. A broad category of musical genres that includes blues, gospel, folk, early country music, bluegrass, old time, cajun, western swing, polka, Tex-Mex, and other styles of nonclassical music.

rose. See rosette.

rosette. The ornamental inlay around the sound hole of an acoustic guitar, lute, or mandolin.

rosin. A sticky substance that is put on the hair of a bow to increase friction.

roto toms. A shell-less drum with a metal rim that can be turned to tighten or loosen the head in order to lower or raise the pitch.

rotoverb. An early stompbox guitar processor that mimicked the sound of a Leslie rotating speaker. Nils Lofgren used this effect frequently in his early career.

rough mix. A preliminary recording mix of a song or composition made prior to a final mix and mastering.

round. A circle canon, usually vocal, at the unison.

rounded binary. A two-section musical form in which the opening "a" section returns at the end of the second section to "round off" the form; e.g., aa baba. Also called "minuet form."

round wound. With a guitar or other string instrument, referring to a string that has a round wire wrapped around a core.

royalties. Monies paid to a licensor by a licensee for the use of intellectual property.

RPM. Revolutions per minute.

rubato [It.]. Flexible in tempo.

rudeboy. A 1960s Jamaican music genre related to ska and reggae and characterized by aggressive lyrics and themes of alienation.

rudiments. (1) The basic skills of a discipline or practice. (2) The basic drum strokes.

ruff. A drum stroke with two grace notes preceding an accented note.

ruhig [Ger.]. Quietly.

rumba. An Afro-Cuban dance with syncopated rhythms.

rumble. Low frequency noise often caused by mechanical devices such as air conditioners, which can mar a recording.

run. A group of scalar notes usually in a rapid tempo.

running the changes. Jazz slang for improvising.

rushing. Playing ahead of the beat.

S. Abbr. for soprano.

Sa. The Indian solfège syllable for the tonic note of a scale. Equivalent to the Western Do.

SA. Abbr. for soprano and alto.

SAB. Abbr. for soprano, alto, bass.

SACEM. Société des auteurs, compositeurs, et éditeurs de musique, a French rights society representing original authors, composers, and publishers.

sackbut. A predecessor of the trombone.

saddle. See bridge piece.

saite [Fr.]. String.

salsa. A fast Latin American dance developed in Cuba in the 1940s, which blends charanga with jazz.

saltando [It.]. Bounced bow stroke.

saltbox. A noise-making instrument used by clowns in the eighteenth century.

samaai. An Egyptian 10/8 rhythmic cycle.

samba. An energetic Brazilian dance and music style in 2/4 meter with roots in African music and dance.

samba school. A Brazilian community club devoted to the practice and performance of samba.

sample. (1) A piece of digitally recorded audio. (2) To record an instrument or unique sound for use in an audio project. (3) A unit of digitally recorded sound.

sample accurate. A parameter's or processor's ability to have a resolution as refined as the sample rate; e.g., when using a sampling rate of 48 kHz, the sample accuracy will be 1/48,000 of a second.

sample library. A collection of usually short recordings (samples) that are often catalogued by subject; e.g., acoustic guitar samples.

sample rate. The number of times per second that a digital recorder is recording sound; e.g., CDs are recorded at 44,100 samples (i.e., 44.1 kHz) per second.

sample replacement. A digital editing technique in which real recorded instruments are replaced or enhanced with samples. The technique can also be used in reverse by using samples as guides for real instruments to overdub or supplement.

sanctus. The fourth section of the Roman Catholic mass.

sans [Fr.]. Without.

sarabande. A slow, regal dance of Spanish origin, in triple meter.

sarangi. A bowed Indian string instrument with three primary strings and numerous sympathetic strings.

sarod. A North Indian plucked stringed instrument with sympathetic strings.

sarrusophone. A family of double-reed brass instruments invented by French composer and inventor Pierre-Auguste Sarrus in the mid-nineteenth century.

SATB. Soprano, alto, tenor, bass.

saturation. In analog tape recording, the largest amount of magnetism a recording tape can hold without distorting the sound.

sautillé [Fr.]. In string playing, a light, springing, bouncing bow stroke.

saw. See musical saw.

sawtooth wave. A waveform that rises to a peak and then falls, creating a jagged sawtooth shape when viewed on an oscilloscope. Sometimes called "ramp waves."

sax. Abbr. for saxophone.

saxhorn. A three- to five-valve brass instrument invented by Belgian musician and instrument-maker Adolphe Sax in 1840.

saxophone. A metal woodwind instrument invented by Belgian musician and instrument-maker Adolphe Sax in about 1840, with mechanical keys similar to those of the clarinet.

saz. A long-necked Turkish lute.

scale. (1) A set of unduplicated pitches arranged low to high within a one-octave span. (2) See union scale. (3) See scale length.

scale approach. An harmonic or melodic avoid note that should be used only to move stepwise to an adjacent pitch.

scale degree. A specific name and/or number given to a note of a scale in accordance to its melodic function.

scale length. The length from nut to bridge of a string instrument.

scat singing. Improvised jazz singing that uses syllables, nonsense words, and instrument imitation.

Schenkerian analysis. A reductive analytical technique and music theory developed by music theorist Heinrich Schenker in the early twentieth century.

scherzando [It.]. Playfully.

scherzo [It.]. (1) A movement in fast triple meter in symphonies, sonatas, and quartets. (2) A light, humorous musical composition, in keeping with "joke," the literal meaning of scherzo.

Schillinger system. A system of music composition that employs mathematics and formulas. The system was developed by Joseph Schillinger in the mid-twentieth century and was championed and taught by Lawrence Berk, the founder of Berklee College of Music. Berklee College of Music was initially named the Schillinger House.

schleppend [Ger.]. Dragging.

schnell [Ger.]. Fast.

SCI. Society of Composers, Inc.

SCL. (1) Society of Composers and Lyricists. (2) Southeastern Composers League.

scoop. Sliding into a note with a portamento instead of a clean articulation.

scordatura [It.]. (1) Alternate tuning. (2) Tuning an instrument to other than its typical tuning. On a guitar, also called "cross tuning" or "open tuning."

score. (1) To orchestrate music. (2) A notated book of a piece of music that includes all the instruments of an ensemble. (3) A music manuscript.

score optimization. A process of deleting empty staves from a large score.

score paper. Paper set up with multiple staves and used for music writing.

score reading. Playing and reducing a large score, such as an orchestra score, on a piano by sight.

score to picture. Create and write music for visual media.

Scotch snap. A rhythmic figure of a sixteenth note followed by a dotted eighth. Also called a "catch."

SCPP. Société Civile des Producteurs Phonographiques, a French performance rights society that collects fees from sound-recording and music-video users and distributes the fees to copyright holders.

scratch. (1) A stroke in playing the turntable. (2) See scratch vocal. (3) A small amount of money.

scratch guard. See pick guard.

scratch plate. See pick guard.

scratch track. A preliminary or informal recording.

scratch vocal. A vocal recorded to serve as a guide, which will be removed later and replaced with a cleaner, better version.

screamo. An aggressive, chaotic musical style that evolved from emo and hardcore.

SDM. Subdominant minor.

S. Dr. Abbr. for snare drum.

sea chanty. A song, often in 6/8 meter, sung by or about sailors and sailing.

secco. [It.]. Dryly.

second. (1) The musical interval between two adjacent tones; e.g., C to D, E♭ to F♯, etc. (2) A group of instruments or voices below the top group; e.g., second violins.

Second Viennese School. Early twentieth-century Expressionist and serial composers Arnold Schoenberg, Anton Webern, and Alban Berg.

section figures. Musical motifs, often background, played by a section, such as brass, in soli.

section solo. A melody played in unison or in harmony by all members of an instrument group.

secundal. Referring to harmonies constructed using the interval of a second.

segno [It.]. A musical sign that marks a specific place in a score.

segue [It.]. Proceed to.

sehr [Ger.]. Very.

selector. A knob or button on a synth or musical device that chooses a patch or program.

semibreve [Br.]. Whole note.

semi-hollow body. An electric guitar with the body shape and open cavity of an acoustic guitar, but with only half the depth.

semiquaver [Br.]. Sixteenth note.

semitone. A half-step interval.

semplice [It.]. Simply.

sempre [It.]. Always.

SENA. Stichting ter Exploitatie van Naburige Rechten, a Dutch rights society that grants licenses and collects fees for performing artists and record producers.

send. An output on a mixer or other audio device that routes a signal to an external processor.

send-off riff. In the first few bars of a chorus, a riff played by a jazz band prior to a soloist improvising over the rest of the chorus.

sensitivity. (1) A MIDI keyboard measure of the amount of pressure required to sound or affect a note. (2) The minimum audio input signal needed for a device to reach its rated output level.

senza [It.]. Without.

septet. (1) A composition for seven performers. (2) A group of seven performers.

septuplet. A group of seven notes played in the span of four or six.

sequence. (1) A musical phrase repeated one or more times at a lower or higher pitch level. See also real sequence and tonal sequence. (2) A hymn of the Roman Catholic Church. (3) A track or composition recorded on a MIDI sequencer.

sequencer. A software or hardware device on which the user can record, edit, and play back MIDI data.

serenade. (1) A romantic song sung to a lover in the evening. (2) A composition evoking the mood of a lover's song.

sereno [It.]. Serenely.

serialism. A method of composition in which the composer creates a row (series) of twelve, or fewer, chromatic pitches and uses them as the basis of harmony and melody.

serious music. See art music.

serpent. An ancient bass wind instrument.

session. (1) A get-together for musicians to jam. (2) A recording engagement. 3) A DAW master document.

session musician. A musician who specializes in playing in recording sessions.

set. A group of songs that a band performs in a segment of a show.

set list. A listing of the group of songs that a band performs in a segment of a show.

set theory. A system for grouping musical pitches for analysis and composition.

seven-string guitar. A guitar with an added string, usually an additional bass string tuned to B.

seventh. (1) The interval between seven diatonic notes. (2) A chord tone seven diatonic notes above the root.

seventh chord. A four-note chord in tertian harmony that includes the fundamental, a third, a fifth, and a seventh.

sevilliana. Spanish flamenco style originating in Seville.

sextet. (1) A composition for six performers. (2) A group of six performers.

sextuplet. A tuplet with six notes in the space of four.

sf. Abbr. for sforzando.

sforzando [It.]. Forced. Suddenly heavily accented.

SFX. Abbr. for special effects, sound effects.

sfz. Abbr. for sforzando.

Sh. Abbr. for shaker.

shake. A trill.

shaker. A percussion instrument that rattles when shaken.

shamisen. A three-stringed, plucked Japanese instrument.

shanty. See sea chanty.

shape note. An early American and English system of music notation in which the shape of the note indicates the pitch to be sung. Also known as "fasola."

sharp. (1) A marking (♯) that indicates a note is to be played one half step higher. (2) Above the pitch.

♯

shawm. A double-reed Medieval woodwind instrument that is a predecessor of the oboe.

shed. (1) To practice one's instrument. (2) To learn a tune.

sheng. A Chinese free-reed mouth organ constructed from a set of bamboo pipes.

shielded cable. Cable that has been insulated to eliminate or attenuate noise and is used to connect instruments, audio equipment, and microphones.

shift. A hand position movement up or down the neck of a stringed instrument such as a violin or guitar.

shimmy. A fast World War I–era ragtime dance.

sho. A Japanese sheng.

shofar. An ancient Jewish trumpet made from a ram's horn.

short score. See reduced score.

shout chorus. A climactic section near or at the end of a jazz big band arrangement during which the entire band plays.

shred. A metal guitar playing style that emphasizes fast, virtuoso passage work and/or sweep picking.

shuffle. A playing style in which the underlying supportive rhythm is somewhere between dotted-eighth/sixteenth and swing triplets, with a strong backbeat.

Si. (1) The solfège syllable indicating the raised sixth degree of a major or minor scale. (2) The note B in fixed Do solfège.

SIAE. Italian Society of Authors and Publishers, a rights society that grants licenses to and collects fees from creators and producers of intellectual works.

Sibelius. Music notation software.

sibilance. High-frequency content in sounds such as "sh" and "s."

siciliana. An Italian dance in 6/8 or 12/8 meter of a moderate tempo.

sideband. The frequency, or frequencies, that result(s) when a waveform is modulated by a second, or by multiple, waveform(s).

sidechain. A control input that is triggered by an external signal.

side drum. A snare drum.

sight-reading. Playing or singing previously unseen notated music without rehearsal.

sight singing. Unrehearsed, and usually unaccompanied, singing of notated music.

signal. An electrical impulse.

signal flow. The route that a signal takes in going through audio equipment.

signal horn. A bugle.

signal processor. A device that alters a signal to create compression, reverb, or various other effects.

signal-to-noise ratio. The measure of noise relative to the level of a signal.

signature. Indication at the beginning of a staff showing key and meter.

silent movie. A film made without an embedded soundtrack.

silounds. Sounds that occur during silent periods in a composition.

sim. Abbr. for simile.

similar motion. See parallel motion.

simile [It.]. In the same manner.

simple meter. A time signature that is divisible by two; e.g., 2/4, 4/4.

sine wave. A waveform that has no overtones and is cyclic and continuous.

sinfonia. A Baroque-period Italian orchestral piece composed as an introduction to a larger work.

sinfonietta. A chamber orchestra.

sing. To make music with the voice.

singer-songwriter. A vocal performer who composes original songs and often accompanies himself or herself on guitar or piano.

singing saw. See musical saw.

single-note comping. A repeating single-note pattern or riff that accompanies a melody.

sinistra [It.]. Left (referring to the left hand).

sistrum. A metal rattle of Egyptian origin.

sitar. A plucked string instrument with many sympathetic strings, used in classical Indian music.

six-four chord. A triad with its fifth in the bass (second inversion).

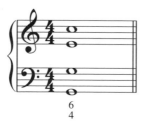

six-string. Guitar.

six-string bass. An electric bass guitar with six strings, rather than the usual four, most often with added low B and high C strings.

sixteenth note. One fourth of the value of a quarter note.

sixteenth rest. One fourth of the value of a quarter rest.

sixth. (1) An interval of six diatonic notes. (2) A chord tone six diatonic notes above the root.

sixth chord. A four-note chord that includes the fundamental, a third, a fifth, and a sixth.

six-three chord. A triad with its third in the bass (first inversion).

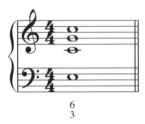

sizzle cymbal. A suspended cymbal with rivets that create a buzzing and sizzling effect when struck.

ska. An upbeat Jamaican popular dance-music style that was a precursor to reggae.

skiffle. A 1950s British popular music style, influenced by American jazz, blues, and country music.

skip. (1) Melodic motion larger than a step. (2) An unwanted jump made by the tonearm of a vinyl record player. (3) A purposeful technique, either digital or analog, that imitates a tonearm skip. (4) A ghosted note on the third tuplet of a beat.

slack-key guitar. See Hawaiian slack-key guitar.

slapback. A signal processing effect that creates a single echo.

slap bass. A style of bass playing in which the strings are played with a variety of percussive fingering techniques instead of being plucked with the fingers or with a pick.

slash chord. A chord with its intended bass note under the slash. Thus, implying an inversion or nonchord tone in the bass (C/E or C/D♭).

slash mark. See slash notation or caesura.

slash notation. (1) Marks attached to stems to indicate the chord rhythm or drum kicks. (2) Marks on a staff indicating the beat; e.g., four slash marks in a bar of 4/4. Often used to indicate that a drummer or rhythm section player is to continue playing the appropriate groove.

slave. In computer and electronic music, an application or device that is controlled by a master application or device.

sleigh bells. A shaken percussion instrument consisting of small metal bells attached to a leather strap.

slendro scale. A five-note Indonesian scale used in gamelan music. See Scales in the Appendix.

slide. (1) A tubular piece of metal or glass that is placed on a fretting finger so that it can glide across the neck to play notes. (2) A long, U-shaped, metal tuning device, such as on a trombone. (3) A glissando or portamento.

slide guitar. A technique of playing the guitar with a tubular slide on the fretting fingers or with another implement that glides across the strings creating glissandi between notes.

slide trumpet. A trumpet equipped with a slide rather than valves.

slip cueing. A DJ technique of starting a record at an exact point by placing the needle on the desired spot while allowing the turntable to spin beneath the record until it is ready to be played.

slit drum. See log drum.

slow change blues. A blues progression that waits until the fifth measure to move to the IV chord.

slur. (1) A curved line showing that the notes underneath or over the line are to be played as a unified phrase. (2) A curved line showing that the notes underneath or over the line are to be played in a single bow stroke. (3) A curved line showing that the notes underneath or over the line are to be played or sung in one breath without individual articulations.

smear. A bend up to a note from underneath.

smooth jazz. A light form of jazz that has easy grooves and limited dissonance.

smorzando [It.]. Dying away.

SMPTE time code. A synchronization time code developed by the Society of Motion Picture and Television Engineers.

snap pizz. See Bartók pizzicato.

snare drum. A double-headed drum, typically played with sticks or brushes, which has vibrating strings pressed against the bottom head that create a buzzing sound.

soft key. A programmable button or key on a computer or digital device that can be assigned for various tasks.

soft knee. A compressor setting that creates a gradual onset of compression.

soft pedal. The left-most pedal on an acoustic piano that softens the sound by moving the hammers so that they strike only two of the three strings in the middle register of a piano. Also called an "una corda pedal."

softsynth. A software music synthesizer that emulates a hardware synthesizer.

Sol. (1) The solfège syllable for the fifth note of the major scale. (2) The note G in fixed Do solfège.

solfège. Various systems used for sight-reading and learning music in which syllables are assigned to scale degrees. The diatonic major key solfège syllables are: Do, Re, Mi, Fa, Sol, La, Ti, Do.

solfeggio. See solfège.

soli [It.]. All together, for all.

solid body. A guitar or bass whose main structure is solid without a resonating cavity. Solid body instruments were developed to avoid the feedback that came from amplifying hollow-body guitars.

solmization. (1) A method invented by Medieval Italian theorist and choral director Guido d'Arezzo for teaching and learning intervals and scales. (2) Singing using solfège syllables.

solo. (1) For one player, alone. (2) Improvisation by a single player in a song. Usually over chord changes. (3) A piece for a single instrument or a single instrument with accompaniment. (4) A button on a hardware or software mixer that mutes all other tracks.

solo break. A short instrumental solo in a jazz tune, played while other members of the band rest.

solo-tone mute. On brass instruments, a long straight mute that accentuates high frequencies.

son. (1) A Cuban music genre that emerged in the 1930s and mixes African rhythms with Spanish canción. (2) A clave pattern.

sonata. A classical music composition for solo instrument or solo instrument with accompaniment, usually in three or four contrasting movements.

sonata-allegro form. A classical music form that consists of an exposition, a development, and a recapitulation, in which the exposition is repeated and a coda often follows the recapitulation.

sonatina. A short sonata, often designed for instruction.

song. Lyrics or text set to music. Usually in a simple formal structure.

song cycle. A set of songs united by a common theme.

song form. In classical music, a simple ABA form. Also known as "ternary form."

sopra [It.]. Above. (e.g., come sopra, as above).

sopranino saxophone. The highest pitched member of the saxophone family with a range of D♭4 to G♭6.

soprano. (1) The highest of the female voice types, with a typical range of C4 to C6. (2) High in pitch.

soprano clef. A moveable C clef with middle C on the first line of the staff.

soprano saxophone. The second highest pitched member of the saxophone family, with a range of A♭3 to E♭6.

sord. See sordino.

sordino [It.]. A mute.

sorrow song. African American slave song that expresses feelings of loss and oppression.

sostenuto [It.]. Sustained.

sostenuto pedal. A piano or keyboard foot pedal that sustains only the notes that are being held down when the pedal is depressed.

sotto [It.]. Under.

sotto voce. [It.]. Whispered.

soukous. A music and dance style from the Democratic Republic of the Congo (formerly Zaire).

soul. A genre of American popular music that emerged in the 1950s and 1960s and blended elements of R&B, gospel, and jazz.

sound-alike. A song or composition that is intended to sound very similar to another, usually very well-known or popular piece of music.

sound bank. A group of stored sounds or patches in a digital keyboard, sequencer, or synthesizer.

soundboard. A resonant piece of wood behind or below the strings of a piano and various other instruments, which assists in amplifying the sound.

sound design. Creation of sounds and special effects through music synthesis.

sound designer. (1) A person who creates sounds using synthesis techniques. (2) A person who creates special effects for movies and other media.

Sound Designer. A 1990s digital audio editing program.

sound hole. An opening in the face of many stringed instruments, which assists in dispersing the sound.

sound isolation. Soundproofing an environment, especially in recording, to prevent sound from spilling from one area into another.

sound mass. Thick bands of pitches, sometimes microtonal, used in composition and orchestration.

sound module. A digital audio device that houses sound samples, which can be triggered by a keyboard or sequencer.

sound post. A stick wedged in a violin, viola, cello, or bass and underneath the bridge to conduct vibration into the instrument.

soundproof. To construct in such a way as to block out sound.

sound separation. (1) The process of giving different instruments or frequencies their individual sonic space in a mix. (2) The process of extracting a specific instrument or voice from a recording.

sound stage. (1) An sound-isolated space dedicated to recording music, dialog, or sound effects. (2) The virtual space created in a digital recording.

sound synthesis. The process and technique of creating waveforms that can be electronically turned in to sound.

soundtrack. (1) The music portion of a film. (2) A recording of music from a film, musical, or television show.

source cue. See source music.

source music. Music in a film or television show that is part of the scene; e.g., a piano player in a bar or a radio playing in a room. Also known as a "source cue."

source scales. Scales that are used as the source of harmony in composition, arranging, and improvisation.

sourdine [Fr.]. A mute.

sousaphone. A marching tuba with coiled tubing and a forward facing bell. Named for John Philip Sousa, American bandleader and "march king" of the late nineteenth and early twentieth century.

southern rock. A subgenre of American rock music that blends country music, blues, and rock and roll.

space. (1) The area between two lines on a staff or between ledger lines. (2) Sonic area in a mix created with EQ and panning. (3) Sonic area of an arrangement created through register and timbre.

space music. (1) Electronic music that emulates the vastness and openness of outer space through sparse motion and a heavily reverbed sonic environment. (2) An art music subgenre that utilizes physical space, including the placement of performers and audience, as a compositional element.

spacing. (1) The vertical arrangement of the notes of a chord. (2) The alignment of notes and other written elements on a score or part.

Spanish guitar. See classical guitar.

Spanish reggae. See reggaeton.

spatial modulation. The movement of sound evenly through three-dimensional space from one location to another.

S/PDIF. Sony/Philips Digital Interface Format.

speaker. See loudspeaker.

speaker cabinet. An enclosure that holds one or more loudspeakers.

special function. A dominant seventh chord whose root does not resolve down by fifth or by half step.

species counterpoint. A method of teaching the art of counterpoint put forward by Austrian composer and theorist Johann Joseph Fux in his book *Gradus ad Parnassum* (1725). There are five species of counterpoint: note against note; two notes against one; four notes against one; ligatures (tied notes/suspensions); mixed counterpoint using the first four species.

spectral music. A 1970s composition method that used the frequency spectrum of a sound as compositional material.

spectrum. A view of all of the frequency components of a waveform.

speed metal. A fast, virtuosic and gritty subgenre of heavy metal music that emerged in the late 1970s.

speed picking. See sweep picking.

spiccatto [It.]. With a bouncing bow.

spill. (1) A woodwind and brass technique in which a note is followed by a rapid diatonic or chromatic downward fall. (2) See bleed.

spinet. (1) A small framed indirect-action piano with horizontal strings. (2) A type of small harpsichord.

spirito [It.]. With spirit.

spiritual. A religious song sung or composed by black slaves in the southern United States.

SPL. Sound pressure level.

splash cymbal. A small suspended cymbal that creates the sound of a splash when struck.

splice. To cut and paste together a section of magnetic audio tape.

splicer. An instrument used to cut and paste together segments of magnetic recording tape.

split keyboard. A synthesizer keyboard divided into two parts, each of which is assigned a different sound or patch.

split screen. A video screen that can display two separate images simultaneously.

spotting. The process of selecting where music is to be used in or composed for a film or visual media project.

spread voicing. A chord voicing, not in close position, that is built from the bottom up.

Sprechstimme [Ger.]. Half-sung, half-spoken voice.

springing bow. A bounced bow technique used by string players.

spring reverb. An electronic reverb effect created by sending an audio signal though a spring or group of springs.

square dance. A folk-style couples' dance often danced in a square formation.

square time. 4/4 or 2/4 meter.

square wave. A pulse wave with equal positive and negative energy whose cyclical shape, when viewed on an oscilloscope, is that of a square.

squeezebox. Accordion.

SSA. Soprano I, soprano II, alto I.

SSAA. Soprano I, soprano II, alto I, alto II.

S. Sax. Abbr. for soprano saxophone.

stab. (1) A short, sudden loud note. (2) In turntable technique, a short, powerful burst of sound.

staccato [It.]. Detached, short.

staccato mark. A dot placed with a notehead indicating a short articulation.

stack. (1) A layered amplifier that consists of one or more speaker cabinets with an amp head placed on top. (2) An extended chord constructed by placing one or more chords above it.

stadium rock. See arena rock.

stage monitor. A monitor speaker, often wedge-shaped, placed on the stage to allow performers to hear themselves in the mix.

standalone. Software or hardware that does not require support from outside of itself.

standard. A popular song that has become a part of a repertoire. See jazz standard.

standing wave. A repeating wave that is caused by sound reflecting back and forth between two parallel surfaces.

stand-up bass. See contrabass.

stanza. See verse.

St. Bs. Abbr. for string bass.

steam calliope. See calliope.

steam organ. See calliope.

steam piano. See calliope.

steel band. An ensemble that features steel drums.

steel drum. A bright-sounding, resonant percussion instrument native to Trinidad and played with mallets, which is constructed from metal barrels whose tops have been worked into sections that sound distinct notes.

steel guitar. (1) A guitar of Hawaiian origin that is played horizontally by sliding a metal bar across the strings to change the pitch while plucking the strings with the nonslide hand. (2) The method of playing a guitar with a metal slide. (3) A guitar, such as a lap steel guitar, that is specifically built to play in the steel guitar fashion.

Steel Str. Gtr. Abbr. for steel-string guitar.

steel-string guitar. An acoustic guitar with metal strings. Most often played with a pick.

Steg [Ger.]. Bridge (e.g., am steg, bowed at the bridge).

stem. (1) A vertical line attached to a notehead. (2) One of the individual tracks or sound files that is part of a mix or larger work.

step. Movement to the next letter-named note; e.g., C to D, F♯ to G, etc.

step progression. A motive, phrase, or series of chords that moves stepwise as a unit.

step time. (1) One note, chord, or rhythm at a time. (2) To input MIDI notes or information into a sequencer in non-real time, one note, chord, or rhythm at a time.

step-time mode. A mode in a MIDI sequencer that allows for step-time input.

stereo. (1) Mixed to two independent channels. (2) A hi-fi phonograph.

sticking. Percussion and drum-set stick technique.

sticks. A pair of hard-tipped mallets used for playing drums and other percussion instruments.

Stks. Abbr. for sticks.

stochastic. (1) Indeterminate. (2) Created using the element of chance.

stochastic music. Music created using elements of chance.

stompbox. See effects pedal.

stop. (1) To place a finger on a string of a string instrument. (2) A set of organ pipes. (3) A knob on an organ that admits or stops airflow into a specific pipe or pipes.

stop-time. Rhythm section hits on the downbeats or other designated beats struck while a soloist continues playing.

straight ahead. A pure and simple groove with only small amounts of syncopation and frills.

straight-eighth jazz. Jazz music without swing eighth notes.

straight eighths. A direction in a jazz score to not swing the eighth notes.

straight mute. A mute for brass instruments that produces a nasal, metallic tone.

strain. A section of a tune, usually eight bars.

Stratocaster. A famous solid-body electric guitar made by Fender.

streamer. A colored vertical line that crosses the screen followed by a flash (punch), used as a cue in a film scoring. See punches and also punches and streamers.

streaming. Delivering data as a flow rather than in packets.

streaming cartridge. A digital tape-storage device developed in the 1980s.

street funk. A style of urban hip-hop dancing often accompanied by boom boxes or various percussion instruments.

street organ. A bellows-driven, cranked, free-reed hand organ.

stretto [It.]. Contracted, overlapping entries in a fugue.

stride piano. An East Coast style of piano playing developed in the 1920s, featuring large leaps in the left hand.

string. (1) A long, thin cord made of metal, nylon, or gut, which is attached to a frame and is plucked or bowed. (2) An instrument of the string family.

string bass. See contrabass.

stringendo [It.]. Quicken in tempo.

string quartet. (1) An ensemble consisting of two violins, a viola, and a cello. (2) An ensemble consisting of any four stringed instruments.

string quintet. (1) An ensemble consisting of two violins, a viola, a cello, and a bass. (2) An ensemble consisting of any five stringed instruments.

strings. (1) The violin, viola, cello, and bass sections of an orchestra. (2) A group of stringed instruments. (3) The plucked or bowed cords attached to a stringed instrument.

string trio. (1) An ensemble consisting of a violin, a viola, and a cello. (2) An ensemble consisting of any three stringed instruments.

stroke. (1) A percussion mallet or stick technique for striking an instrument. (2) A specific motion made with the bow of a stringed instrument.

strophic. Referring to vocal music constructed in verses in which the text changes but the music stays essentially the same.

strum. A stringed-instrument playing technique of running the fingers or a pick across the strings to create an arpeggio.

studio orchestra. (1) A chamber ensemble or symphony orchestra employed to record music. (2) An orchestra or ensemble that records music.

study score. A reduced-size music manuscript of a large composition, which is meant for learning or studying.

Sturm und Drang [Ger.]. Literally, storm and stress. A late eigthteenth-century music and literature movement.

stutter. A digital audio effect achieved by cutting audio into small bits and then repeating the edits to make a stuttering sound. Also called a "glitch."

sub. Abbr. for subwoofer.

sub-bass. A sixteen- or thirty-two-foot organ stop.

sub-bass clef. A moveable bass (F) clef where F3 is on the top line of the staff.

subcontrabass saxophone. A very low-pitched member of the saxophone family that Adolphe Sax imagined but did not build. It is in the key of B♭ and sounds an octave below the bass saxophone.

subdominant. (1) The fourth degree of a major or minor scale. (2) A key area or harmony that is built on the fourth degree of a major or minor scale.

subdominant cadence. See plagal cadence.

subdominant minor partners. Subdominant minor to dominant pairings, such as IImi7♭5 moving to V7.

subito [It.]. Suddenly.

subject. (1) The primary theme in a fugue, which becomes the basis for imitation. (2) The main melody that a composition is based on.

submediant. (1) The sixth degree of a major or minor scale that is a third below tonic. (2) A key area or harmony that is built on the sixth degree of a major or minor scale.

submix. A group of instruments or audio tracks inserted as a solo or stereo track into the main mix.

suboctave. The octave below a note.

subsonic. Traveling slower than the speed of sound.

substitute dominant. A dominant seventh chord that replaces another dominant seventh chord that shares the same tritone. The roots of the two chords will be a tritone apart. Also known as a "tritone substitution."

substitution. (1) A chord that replaces another chord in an arrangement or improvisation, usually with a similar function. (2) A replacement chord that reharmonizes a melody.

subtonic. See leading tone.

subtractive synthesis. A synthesis technique in which frequency components of a rich wave are subtracted to create a new wave (sound).

sub V. Abbr. for substitute dominant.

subwoofer. A loudspeaker designed to reproduce low frequencies.

suite. A set of short instrumental pieces, often utilizing dance forms.

sul [It.]. On.

sul pont [It.]. On the bridge. A performance indication to bow the strings close to or on the bridge of a string instrument.

sul tasto [It.]. On the fingerboard. A performance indication to bow the strings on the fingerboard of a string instrument.

summation tone. See combination tone.

superdominant. (1) The sixth degree of a major or minor scale. (2) A key area or harmony that is built on the sixth degree of a major or minor scale. Also known as submediant.

super Locrian scale. See Scales in the Appendix.

superset. In set theory, a set that contains one or more other sets.

supertonic. (1) The second degree of a major or minor scale. (2) A key area or harmony that is built on the second degree of a major or minor scale.

sur [Fr.]. On.

surdo. A traditional large bass drum used in Brazilian samba.

surf music. A subgenre of popular music from the 1960s, using cultural themes based on a Southern California surfing lifestyle.

surf rock. See surf music.

sur la touche. [Fr.]. Bowed on the fingerboard.

surprise cadence. An unexpected resolution of a cadence.

surround sound. A playback system with multiple (three or more) loudspeakers placed around a listener or audience.

sus2 chord. A triad in which the third is replaced by a second.

sus4 chord. A triad in which the third of the chord is replaced by a fourth.

Sus. C. Abbr. for suspended cymbal.

suspended cymbal. A single cymbal that is held or hung on a stand.

suspension. (1) A nonchord tone occurring in a triad or seventh chord, prepared by common tone, and resolved by step. (2) A dissonance between two pitches in which the lower or upper tone resolves by step into a consonance.

sustain. (1) To prolong a note. (2) A device that prolongs a note. (3) The third portion of an ADSR envelope. (4) A MIDI continuous controller message that prolongs a note.

sustain pedal. (1) A foot pedal on an acoustic piano that lifts the dampers from the strings, allowing them to ring out until the pedal is released or the sound decays. (2) A pedal on a keyboard that prolongs the sound, emulating a piano sustain pedal.

Suzuki method. A primarily rote teaching method, that emphasizes "right environment." Developed by Shinichi Suzuki for young children learning to play the violin and then later applied to other instruments.

sweep picking. A guitar picking technique that utilizes both hands to create seamless and fast runs of notes.

sweetening. Adding reverb and processing to a track or sound file.

swell. (1) Part of a pipe organ, a set of pipes enclosed in a box with shutters that can be opened and closed to create a change in dynamics. (2) A crescendo and immediate decrescendo.

swing. (1) A style of jazz that emerged in the 1930s, featuring walking bass lines, harmonies often with added sixth chords, and singable melodies with swing eighths. (2) A style indication to have walking bass and swing eighths.

swing eighths. Jazz-style eighth notes in which the first of a pair is held longer than the second. Sometimes notated as a dotted-eighth note followed by a sixteenth note, or as an eighth-note triplet with the first two eighths tied.

swing era. Starting in the 1930s, a period when popular American music was dominated by big bands.

swunk. A musical mixture/style combining swing and funk.

symmetrical diminished scale. See octatonic scale and Scales in the Appendix.

symmetric dominant scale. See Scales in the Appendix.

sympathetic strings. Strings on a stringed instrument that are meant to be excited into vibration by notes played on the stopped or bowed melody strings, thereby creating added resonance and sonic complexity.

sympathetic vibration. A vibration caused by another object vibrating at the same frequency.

symphonic band. See concert band.

symphony. (1) A large orchestra that is made up of woodwinds, brass, percussion, and string sections. (2) A composition for a symphony orchestra.

Syn. Abbr. for synthesizer.

sync. See synchronization.

synchronization. Connecting two or more devices so they will work together or as one unit.

synchronized music. Music with specific timings written for a film.

Synclavier. A digital synthesizer and sampler introduced by New England Digital Corporation in 1975.

sync license. See music synchronization license.

syncopation. Accenting a normally weak beat (offbeat) or pulse.

sync points. (1) Points in a film or other visual media indicating where music or sound are to begin. (2) Points in a free-timed composition where elements align.

synth. Short for synthesizer.

synthesizer. An electronic and/or digital instrument with which a user can create and alter sounds.

synthpop. A pop music subgenre in which synthesizers are used extensively.

syrinx. See panpipes.

sys-ex. MIDI system exclusive data.

system. A collection of two or more connected staves.

systematic music. See minimalism.

T. Abbr. for tenor.

taarab. Popular East African music style.

tab. See tablature.

tabla. A pair of drums played with the fingers and palms in Indian classical music.

tablature. Musical notation for fretted string instruments, which indicates the string and fret to be played.

table [Fr.]. Board (e.g., Pres de la table, near the sounding board).

table canon. See mirror canon.

tablet. A flat, one-piece, touchscreen computer.

tabor. A small Medieval folk drum.

tacet [It.]. (1) Literally, silent. (2) Do not play.

Tafelmusik [Ger.]. (1) Literally, table music. (2) Music played at late-Renaissance banquets and feasts.

tag. A section of music added on to the end of a song. Similar to a coda in classical music.

tag ending. See tag.

tail. The end portion of an audio recording tape.

tails. A chord or note that diminuendos at the end of a cue.

tal. A time cycle in Indian classical music.

tala. A constant repeating rhythm in an isorhythmic motet.

talea. The repeating rhythm in an isorhythmic motet.

talent. (1) A person with special musical ability. (2) A performing artist.

talent agent. See agent and booking agent.

talking drum. An hourglass-shaped drum with the two heads connected by strings, which, when squeezed, cause the pitch to rise.

tallone [It.]. Frog (of the bow).

talon [Fr.]. Frog (of the bow).

Tamb. Abbr. for tambourine.

tamborim. Small, circular Brazilian frame drum.

tambour. A drum.

tambourine. A small, circular, framed hand drum with thin, jangling, metal plates attached.

tambura. A drone instrument with four strings; used in classical Indian music.

tampoura. See tambura.

tam-tam. A gong.

tango. A popular syncopated Argentinian ballroom dance.

tantan. Modern version of the traditional Brazilian surdo.

tanto [It.]. So much.

tanyata. Mellifluous wind instrument of Russian origin.

tape loop. A small length of analog recording tape that circulates in a tape recorder and creates multiple repetitions.

tape recorder. An electronic device that uses magnetic tape to capture, store, and play back audio.

tapping. A guitar technique in which the picking fingers of an electric guitar or bass player tap on the fretboard and work with the fretting fingers to sound pitches.

tap tempo. A button or other control on a sequencer that allows a user to set a tempo or pulse by tapping.

target chord. A chord chosen by a writer as an important point in a phrase.

tasto [It.]. Fingerboard.

Tb. Abbr. for tuba.

Tbn. Abbr. for trombone.

Te. The solfège syllable for the seventh note of a natural minor scale or lowered seventh of a major scale.

teaser. Introductory music that precedes the opening scene at the start of a film.

techno. A style of electronic dance music that utilizes drum machines and other electronic instruments. There are numerous subgenres associated with techno.

techno-rave. A subgenre of techno music.

tech pop. See electroclash.

techstep. A drum and bass subgenre featuring ethereal soundscapes and futuristic samples.

Tejano. A Tex-Mex musical style.

Telecaster. A twangy electric guitar manufactured by Fender.

telenn. A Breton harp.

teli. Abbr. for Fender Telecaster guitar.

Temp. Bl. Abbr. for temple blocks.

temper. To bring notes into temperament.

temperament. A tuning system in which pure intonation notes are adjusted to fit into one of the tempered tuning systems. See also equal temperament.

template. A preset format in a music application such as a notation or sequencer program.

temple blocks. A percussion instrument made from hollow wood blocks that are struck with mallets or sticks.

tempo. The rate of speed of a piece of music.

tempo map. Tempo changes that are programmed into a sequencer.

tempo mark. A written indication in a score or part of the speed of a piece.

tempo primo [It.]. Original tempo.

temp score. In a film project, previously recorded music that has the desired mood and style and serves as a placeholder until a composer replaces it with an original score.

temp track. (1) A guide track in a mix that will later be rerecorded. (2) See temp score.

teneramente [It.]. Tenderly.

tenor. (1) The highest natural adult male singing voice, with a typical range of C3 to C5. (2) An instrument with approximately the same range as a tenor voice. (3) A viola. (4) The voice that carries the cantus firmus in early polyphony.

tenor clef. A moveable C clef with middle C placed on the fourth line of a staff.

tenor saxophone. The tenor member of the saxophone family in the key of B♭ with a range of A♭2 to E♭5.

tension. A chord tone derived from upper extensions of the basic triadic structure (9, 11, 13). Tensions are usually in the melody and may also occur in inner voices, but never in the bass.

tension substitution. An arranging and performance technique in which a chord tension replaces a chord tone; e.g., 9 replacing 1, or 13 replacing 5.

tenth. An interval of an octave and a third.

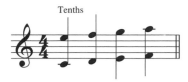

tenuto [It.]. Hold for full value.

ternary. Indicating three parts.

ternary form. A composition consisting of three parts, typically ABA. Also known as "song form" in classical music.

tertian harmony. Harmony constructed in thirds.

tessitura. The pitch range of an instrument or voice.

test tone. A waveform of a specific frequency and level used to calibrate and test audio equipment.

tetrachord. A set of four notes.

tetrad. A four-note chord.

Tex-Mex. A genre of music that arose along the border of Texas and Mexico and has influences from pop, rock, mariachi, and Mexican folk music.

text painting. Using musical gestures, melodies, rhythms, and harmonies to mirror the words; e.g., using a fast, upward moving scale to set the words "running quickly up."

texture. A musical soundscape consisting of pitch, timbre, rhythmic complexity, and density.

theme. The primary musical motive or melody of a composition.

theme and variations. A composition in which a stated theme is redressed in contrasting sections with varying harmonies and melodic permutations.

theme song. A song or instrumental composition that serves as the opening music for a television, radio, or other serialized show or movie.

theorbo. A large Renaissance lute with two necks.

theory. The study of music fundamentals, notation, harmony, and compositional practices.

theremin. An early electronic instrument with two antennas invented by Léon Theremin in the early twentieth century. Its wavering pitch and eerie sound made it useful for novel musical effects.

thesis. A strong beat or downbeat.

third. (1) An interval of three diatonic notes. (2) A chord tone three diatonic notes above the root.

third-stream jazz. A jazz genre that emerged in the 1950s and combined classical music with improvised jazz.

thirteenth. (1) The interval of an octave and a sixth. (2) A chord tone an octave and a sixth above the root.

thirty-second note. One eighth of the value of a quarter note.

thirty-second rest. One eighth of the value of a quarter rest.

thorough bass. See basso continuo.

thrash. A fast and aggressive subgenre of heavy metal music.

through-composed. A compositional form in which sections do not return or repeat.

thru box. A hardware device that receives and distributes multiple MIDI-thru messages.

thumb piano. See mbira.

thumb position. A left-hand position high on the neck of a cello or bass in which the thumb depresses the string, creating a moveable nut.

thumb rest. See finger rest.

Ti. The solfège syllable for the seventh note of a major scale.

tick. A unit of time used in MIDI. In the MIDI protocol, the length of a tick is defined by the time format.

tie. A curved notation mark joining two notes of the same pitch and indicating that the two notes are to be held for their combined duration.

tierce de picardie [Fr.]. See Picardy third.

Timb. Abbr. for timbales.

timbales. Cuban drums, most often in pairs with metal shells, that are played with sticks.

timbre. A tone's color and quality.

timbre variation. A technique in jazz improvisation and arranging in which the performer changes the tone color of notes with mutes, growls, and other devices and performance techniques.

time. (1) Meter. (2) Tempo. (3) The player's ability to maintain a tempo or groove. (4) A note's duration.

time code. One of the methods (codes) for synchronizing audio to picture as well as for synchronizing MIDI and digital devices. See also SMPTE time code.

time compression. Processing a sound file to make it shorter in duration without changing its pitch.

time expansion. Processing a sound file to make it longer in duration without changing its pitch.

time-line pattern. In African music, a foundational repeated rhythm that is often asymmetrical.

time signature. A notational symbol that shows both the number of beats in a measure and the note value that represents one beat or pulse.

Time Signature

time-stretching. A digital processing technique in which a segment of audio is lengthened without changing the pitch.

Timp. Abbr. for timpani.

timpani. A large cup-shaped brass or copper drum, played with mallets, which has a head that can be tuned to a specific pitch. Also called a *kettledrum.

tine. A short, rigid wire rod that, when struck, creates a musical tone. Tines created the signature sound of the classic Fender Rhodes electric piano.

tinnitus. A medical condition in which the sufferer hears sounds that are not physically present; e.g., ringing in the ears.

Tin Pan Alley. (1) A group of late nineteenth- and early twentieth-century New York City composers, music publishers, and songwriters who produced a large amount of popular music. (2) Music written in the style of those composers.

tintinnabuli. A style of music created by Estonian composer Arvo Pärt, which features a repeated, arpeggiated tonic chord (the tintinnabular voice). "Tintinnabulum" means "bell" in Latin.

tin whistle. See penny whistle.

tiple. A small Columbian guitar with twelve strings in four courses of three.

tirando. A free stroke in classical guitar playing in which the plucking finger does not come to rest on the next string.

toaster. (1) A computer program for recording and finalizing CDs. (2) A rapper. (3) See also DJ.

toccata. A virtuosic composition for organ or harpsichord that often features fast scalar passages and imitation.

tom-tom. (1) Double-headed drums with no snares, which are part of a drum set. (2) A Native American drum that is played with the hands, mallets, or sticks.

tonal. (1) Music whose harmonies and melodies are built around a major or minor scale. (2) Music that gravitates around a unique pitch.

tonal answer. A comes (answer) in a fugue that conforms to the key and is not an exact transposition.

tonal center. (1) The key of a musical composition. (2) The pitch that a composition is centered on.

tonal interchange. A segment of a progression that temporarily implies a new key but does not establish it with a confirming cadence.

tonality. (1) The key of a piece of music. (2) The concept of notes revolving around a pitch center.

tonal music. Music within a specific tonality. See tonal and tonal center.

tonal sequence. A repetition in a sequence that adheres to the scale and is not an exact transposition of the initial phrase.

tone. (1) A specific note or pitch. (2) The timbre of a note. (3) The interval of a second.

tone cluster. A group of pitches made up of major and minor seconds played simultaneously.

tone color. The timbre of a tone.

tone generator. An electronic device that creates an audio frequency and is often used for testing audio equipment.

tone row. An ordered set of pitches. See also serialism.

tongued. A tongue-articulated note.

tonguing. A wind and brass technique in which the tongue stops the airflow to articulate a note.

tonic. The first note of a scale or key. Also called a keynote.

tonic group. The set of chords in a key that have a tonic function; e.g., I, IIImi, and VImi in a major key.

tonicization. (1) In a piece of music, causing a listener to feel that a pitch is the home base for other pitches to circle around and gravitate to. (2) Causing a pitch other than the original overall tonic to act as a temporary tonic.

Tonmeister [Ger.]. (1) Sound master. (2) A trained musician who has deep knowledge in both music and sound recording. (3) A four-year European degree in sound recording.

top forty. (1) The most popular current music according to the *Billboard* charts. (2) The forty most played and bought songs currently on the *Billboard* charts.

topline. The melody and lyrics added to an existing track.

top-note voicing. Chord voicing constructed down from the top note or melody.

torch song. A song, often very emotional, of unrequited love.

total serialization. A method of serial composition in which all elements of the composition are serialized.

touch. (1) The action of a keyboard instrument. (2) A player's tactile sensitivity on his or her instrument.

touche [Fr.]. Fingerboard.

touch-five harmonic. An artificial harmonic on a string instrument produced by stopping the string with a finger or thumb and gently touching the string with another finger a perfect fifth higher. The resultant harmonic is an octave higher than the touchpoint.

touch-four harmonic. An artificial harmonic on a string instrument produced by stopping the string with a finger or thumb and gently touching the string with another finger a perfect fourth higher. The resultant harmonic is an octave and a perfect fifth higher than the touchpoint.

touch sensitivity. The capability of a synthesizer or keyboard to measure a finger's pressure on a key and respond accordingly.

tout [Fr.]. All.

Tpt. Abbr. for trumpet.

track. (1) An individual song or selection on a CD, vinyl album, or cassette tape. (2) A single channel of a multitrack recording session. (3) A recording section on a magnetic tape. (4) A general term for a recorded piece of music. (5) To record, as in "track vocals."

tracking room. The performing and recording space of a studio that is separate from the control room.

trade fours. Two alternating four-bar solos over the changes with members of a jazz band. Other lengths are also common such as trading eights or trading twos.

trad jazz. Short for "traditional jazz," which refers to music in ragtime, Dixieland, and other earlier styles.

trance. A subgenre of EDM that features loops and repeating melodies, thus creating a trance-like effect.

tranquillo [It.]. Calmly.

transcribe. To write down the melody, chords, and other elements of a song after hearing it played.

transcription. (1) An arrangement of a piece for an ensemble or group, which is different from the original version. (2) A written version of a piece that was produced after hearing it.

transient. A temporary spike or peak in a waveform or audio signal.

transient modulation. A brief change of key that quickly returns to the original key.

transition. (1) A section that links two parts of a song or composition; e.g., of a verse and a chorus. (2) A modulation.

transitional modulation. An ambiguous tonal area that links two keys.

transparent voicing. A sparse, widely spaced harmonic voicing.

transpose. To change music from its original key into a new key.

transposed score. A score in which the music for transposing instruments has been written in their transposed keys.

transverse flute. A flute that is held horizontally.

trap. A fast, synth- and bass-driven style of music that was an outgrowth of the southern U.S. hip-hop scene in the early 2000s.

trap kit. See drum set.

traps. See drum set.

trap set. See drum set.

traurig [Ger.]. Sadly.

Travis picking. A guitar-picking style attributed to mid-twentieth-century American country-and-western guitarist Merle Travis, in which the thumb picks a bass line and the fingers of the same hand fill in syncopations.

treble. (1) Higher frequencies in the audio spectrum. (2) Upper voices. (3) A tone control that increases or attenuates high frequencies of a signal.

tremolo. (1) Fluctuation of a signal's amplitude that creates a wavering sound. (2) A control on an amplifier musical device used to fluctuate a signal's amplitude. (3) Alternating rapidly between two pitches or chords. (4) Repeating a note or chord very rapidly.

tremolo bar. See whammy bar. Technically, although it is often used, "tremolo bar" is incorrect, since tremolo fluctuates the amplitude of a signal, not the pitch.

très [Fr.]. Very.

triad. A three-note chord consisting of a root with intervals of a third and fifth above the root.

triangle. A percussion instrument that is made from a thin metal rod bent into the shape of a triangle and struck with a short metal rod.

triangle wave. A waveform that, when viewed on an oscilloscope, takes on the shape of a triangle.

tribal house. A subgenre of house music, infused with world music. The typical four-on-the-floor patterns are mixed with polyrhythms played on ethnic percussion instruments.

trichord. A set of three notes.

trick canon. See catch.

trill. Rapid alternation of a note with another note a half or whole step higher.

trim. A control on a mixing board that adjusts a channel's initial input gain.

trio. (1) A composition for three performers. (2) A group of three performers.

trio sonata. A Baroque sonata consisting of two upper parts and a basso continuo.

trip-hop. A 1990s subgenre of electronic music that featured elements of soul, funk, and jazz.

triple-A. Adult Album Alternative. See AAA.

triple harp. A Welsh harp with three rows of strings.

triple meter. A time signature with three main beats to the measure.

triplet. Three notes in the space of two.

triple tongue. A triplet wind or brass articulation created by the tongue silently voicing "ta ka ta."

tritone. The interval of an augmented fourth or a diminished fifth.

tritone substitution. Replacing a chord (typically, a dominant seventh chord) with a chord whose root is a tritone above or below the root of the first chord. In dominant seventh chords, the two chords will share the same tritone between the thirds and sevenths. See also substitute dominant.

trombone. A low brass instrument in which the pitch is changed in part by moving a long U-shaped slide that lengthens or shortens to produce the appropriate pitch.

trope. New text or a melisma added to a Medieval plainchant.

troppo [It.]. Too much.

troubadours. Itinerant French poet-musicians of the Medieval period.

trumpet. An oval-shaped brass instrument with a cup-shaped mouthpiece attached to a cylindrical tube that ends with a flared bell. The trumpet family includes trumpets in B♭, C, D, and E♭, as well as piccolo trumpets and bass trumpets.

TRS. Abbr. for a tip, ring, sleeve audio connector.

T. Sax. Abbr. for tenor saxophone.

TTB. Abbr. for a choral group consisting of tenor I, tenor II, bass.

TTBB. Abbr. for a choral group consisting of tenor I, tenor II, bass I, bass II.

tuba. The bass member of the brass family, it is a low-sounding, large instrument that comes in three sizes: F tuba, C tuba, and B♭ tuba.

tube amp. An audio amplifier that has vacuum tubes instead of solid-state circuits.

tubular bells. See chimes.

tubular chimes. See chimes.

tumbao. An Afro-Cuban bass line.

tune. (1) To adjust an instrument or voice to play the correct or desired pitch. (2) A song. (3) A melody.

tuner. (1) A digital device that attaches to an instrument and shows when a string or played pitch is in tune. (2) See tuning peg and tuning head.

tuning. A specific set of notes or intonations to which a musical instrument is tuned.

tuning fork. A two-pronged metal device that, when struck, emits a specific pitch to which instruments may tune.

tuning head. A mechanical device attached to the string of an instrument, which is turned to tighten or loosen the string.

tuning peg. A tapered dowel inserted into the scroll of a violin or other string instrument, which is wrapped with a string and turned to tighten or loosen it.

tuplet. A group of notes of similar duration, which do not divide equally into the subdivisions of a time signature; e.g., a triplet (three in the space of two) or a quintuplet (five in the space of four).

turn. A four- or five-note figure in which a central tone is embellished by a lower and upper neighbor.

turnaround. A progression used at the end of a tune or section that leads back to the beginning of a tune or section.

turntable. A box-shaped device with a revolving platter, tone arm, and needle, used for playing vinyl records.

tutti [It.]. All.

Tuvan throat singing. A technique of overtone singing developed by the Mongol people of Mongolia and Tuva. Also called "Mongolian throat singing."

twelfth. The interval of an octave and a fifth.

twelve-inch single. A vinyl record that is used by DJs and has grooves cut in a wider spacing in order to give it a broader dynamic range.

twelve-string guitar. A guitar with six courses of two strings, of which the lower four courses are tuned in octaves, and the upper two courses are tuned in unison.

twelve-tone music. See serialism.

twelve-tone technique. See serialism.

two-five. A pairing of a chord built on the second degree of a major or minor scale, followed by a dominant seventh chord built on the fifth degree of a major or minor scale.

two step. A fast ballroom dance from the early twentieth-century.

tympani. See timpani.

Uilleann pipes. Irish bellows-blown bagpipes. National bagpipe of Ireland.

ukulele. A guitar-like fretted, four-stringed, plucked instrument originating in Hawaii.

ultra Locrian scale. See Scales in the Appendix.

una corda [It.]. On one string.

una corda pedal. See soft pedal.

unbalanced. Referring to an electric circuit in which the two signal paths are not balanced and therefore could add noise into a system.

underground. Out of the cultural mainstream.

underscore. (1) Original music written to support a movie, television show, or play. (2) To write music that supports a scene in a movie or a television show but without drawing attention to itself.

undertone. Notes created by inverting an overtone.

undertone series. A series of notes created by inverting an overtone series.

unidirectional. A microphone sound-capturing pattern that captures sound from only one direction.

union scale. The minimum amount that a contractor is to pay a musician for a specific service, as determined by the musician's union.

unison. (1) Two tones of identical pitch. (2) When two tones are of identical pitch (as in "in unison"). (3) When two or more musicians play the same melody or note at the same time.

unity gain. A state in which the input and the output signal between two devices is the same.

unmeasured tremolo. Tremolo notes that are not of a specified duration.

un peu [Fr.]. A little.

unrelated key. See distantly related key.

unruhig [Ger.]. Restlessly.

upbeat. (1) The rhythmic pulse (beat) preceding the downbeat of a measure. See pickup. (2) Having a fast tempo.

up-bow. A bow stroke that starts at the tip of the bow and moves towards the frog.

upper neighbor. A nonharmonic tone that is a step above a chord tone.

upper-structure layer. The top notes of a nontraditional chord voicing.

upper-structure triad. A triad that is played over a chord; e.g., 9, ♯11, and 13 over a major seventh chord.

upright bass. See contrabass.

upright piano. A piano with a vertical string box and soundboard and strings that are arranged diagonally.

upsample. To convert digital audio from a lower sample rate to a higher sample rate.

urban blues. American blues music from the 1920s, which was more codified than rural blues forms and was influenced by city life in lyrics and instrumentation, and was also audience focused.

USB. Universal serial bus, a standard for connecting computers and devices.

UST. Upper-structure triad.

Ut. (1) The Guidonian solfège syllable for Do. (2) The French fixed Do solfège syllable for C.

value. The relative duration of a note or rest; e.g., quarter note or a half rest.

valve. On a brass instrument, a mechanism that, when depressed, alters the tubing length, thus making it possible to play a chromatic scale.

valve trombone. A trombone with valves instead of the more usual slide.

vamp. (1) A repeated series of chords or a melody that is repeated until a cue is given to go forward. (2) An improvised introduction.

variable coupling. A mechanical voicing technique in big band writing and arranging in which the lead alto is coupled and alternates with either the second or third trumpet or lead trombone.

variable pitch control. See varispeed control.

variation. (1) A permutation of a melody or chord progression. (2) A single section from a set of variations.

variations. A musical form in which a theme is followed by a set of melodic or harmonic permutations. Also known as "theme and variations."

Variety. A weekly American entertainment magazine.

varispeed control. A control on a tape recorder or its digital equivalent that allows a user to adjust the speed of the take-up reel, causing the pitch to rise or fall. Digital devices can vary the speed (length) of a sound file without altering the pitch.

vaudeville. A late nineteenth- and early twentieth-century variety show that featured popular songs and comedy.

Vc. Abbr. for violoncello (cello).

VCA. Voltage controlled amplifier, an analog synthesis device that controls the level of a sound.

VCF. Voltage controlled filter, an analog synthesis device that controls the harmonic frequency content of a sound.

VCO. Voltage controlled oscillator, an analog synthesis device that controls the frequency of a sound.

vector. In set theory, a six-digit list that represents the number of unique intervals (unison through tritone) found in a given set.

veejay. See VJ.

veena. A South Indian plucked string instrument.

veloce [It.]. Quickly.

velocity. A MIDI signal, measured 0 to 127, that controls how strongly a key or note is struck.

velocity sensitive. A keyboard or other MIDI instrument whose keys read MIDI velocity information.

verb. Short for "reverb."

verse. (1) A section of a song in which the story is presented. Most often followed by a chorus. Also called a "stanza." (2) A solo portion of a sacred anthem.

verse-refrain. A song that has the main title or its signature phrase at the end of each verse.

vertical avoid note. An avoid note in a harmonic structure.

vessel flute. A small wind instrument with an enclosed cavity, historically constructed from clay, although now also made from plastic, glass, and other hard substances.

via [It.]. Take away or off.

via sordino [It.]. Remove mute.

Vib. Abbr. for vibraphone.

vibes. See vibraphone.

vibraharp. See vibraphone.

vibraphone. A pitched percussion instrument with metal bars laid out in the formation of a piano keyboard.

vibraslap. A percussion instrument that consists of a thick, U-shaped, metal wire connecting a wooden ball at one end and a wooden box with rattles at the other.

vibration. Rapid movement of a string or other material, which results in the formation of sound waves.

vibrato. (1) Oscillation of pitch. (2) Technique for rapidly moving the pitch up and down within a narrow range on an instrument or voice to create a wavering effect.

vibrato bar. See whammy bar.

Vibratone. A loudspeaker made by Fender in the 1970s to imitate the sound of a rotating Leslie speaker. The Vibratone was much lighter and did not have a rotating speaker or onboard amplifier.

Vienna Strings. A popular sampled string library.

Viennese School. A group of composers who worked in and around Vienna, Austria, during the Classical period. See also Second Viennese School.

vif [Fr.]. Lively.

vigoroso [It.]. Vigorously.

vihuela. An early Spanish lute.

vinyl. (1) A flat disk made of polyvinyl chloride onto which sound is recorded. (2) A phonograph (gramophone) record.

viol. A family of bowed instruments and a predecessor of the violin family. Viols had frets, six strings, and flat backs, and were played with arched bows.

viola. (1) A four-stringed, bowed, alto member of the violin family whose strings are tuned C3, G3, D4, A4.
(2) A ten-stringed, two-course, Brazilian guitar.
(3) A twelve-stringed Cape Verdean guitar.

viola da braccio [It.]. A member of the viol instrument family, which was played on the arm.

viola da gamba [It.]. A member of the viol instrument family, which was played by holding the instrument between the legs.

viola d'amore [It.]. An unfretted string instrument of the viol family, with a set of sympathetic strings.

violin. A four-stringed, bowed, and plucked instrument, with an unfretted neck attached to a resonating body. The violin's strings are tuned G3, D4, A4, E5, and it has a range of G3 to E7.

violin bass. See Beatle bass.

violoncello. See cello.

violone. A bass member of the viol family.

virelai. A Medieval French form of poetry and music.

virginal. An early Baroque harpsichord with a single choir of transverse strings.

virtual instrument. A computer-hosted software-generated sound that imitates an analog or digital synthesizer, sampler, or an acoustic instrument.

virtual mixer. A software mixer that reproduces the look and functions of a hardware mixer.

vite [Fr.]. Quickly.

vivace [It.]. Lively.

vivo [It.]. Lively.

VJ. A video jockey who introduces new music videos.

Vla. Abbr. for viola.

Vlc. Abbr. for violoncello (cello).

Vln. Abbr. for violin.

vocal. Relating to the voice.

vocal booth. In a studio, an isolated recording space used primarily for tracking vocals.

vocalese. A composition for wordless voice and instruments.

vocalize. To perform vocal exercises.

vocal score. A reduction of a composition for voice(s) and ensemble, arranged for voice(s) and piano.

vocoder. A voice-operated encoder that splits a voice into frequency bands, which in turn are used to filter other sound sources, thus giving the resulting sound the characteristic of talking.

voice. (1) The sound created by the vocal mechanism. (2) An individual part in polyphonic music.

voice exchange. In polyphonic music, the switching of one voice part's role or register with another's.

voice leading. The smooth connection of the individual parts moving from one harmony to another.

voiceover. (1) The voice of an unseen person dubbed in, in a studio, to replace an actor's original speech. (2) A narrative superimposed on a visual media project.

voicing. (1) The arrangement of notes within a chord structure. (2) The tuning and timbre adjustment of organ pipes.

volti subito [It.]. Turn page quickly.

volume. (1) A sound's loudness or signal level. (2) A knob or fader used to control signal level. (3) A storage area or unit on a computer's hard disk.

volume pedal. A foot-controlled potentiometer that, when pressed, increases or decreases loudness.

vox [Lat.]. (1) Voice. (2) Abbr. for voice.

VPL. Video Performance Limited, a rights society representing copyright holders of music videos.

v.s. Abbr. for volti subito.

VU meter. Volume unit meter, used to measure sound pressure level in decibels.

wahrani. Algerian music style featuring a mix of Egyptian sounds.

wah-wah mute. For brass instruments, a metal mute that creates a buzzing sound. Also called a "Harmon mute."

wah-wah pedal. An effects pedal that creates a crying sound by sweep-filtering between low and high frequencies.

walking bass. A steady quarter-note bass line, using mostly stepwise motion and arpeggios, which connects the chords of a jazz or jazz-influenced composition.

walla. In the visual media industry, term for the sound of crowd murmur in the background.

wall of sound. A producing and arranging concept, attributed to Phil Spector, in which the entire sonic space is filled.

waltz. A swirling ballroom dance in triple meter.

warez. Music, video, and software illegally copied from the Internet.

warmth. A sound quality created though enhanced low- and mid-range frequencies.

waschsend [Ger.]. Getting louder.

washboard. A ridged metal laundry board used as a percussion instrument in American roots music.

washtub bass. A plucked bass instrument constructed from a washtub, a broom handle, and a string and used in American roots music.

waterphone. A percussion instrument made from a steel resonator to which bronze rods are attached. When the bronze rods are struck with mallets, water in the resonator enhances the sound of the instrument. Also called an "ocean harp."

WAV. A file extension indicating a Microsoft digital audio file. Also called a "wave file."

wave file. See WAV.

waveform. The periodic envelope shape of a sound.

waveform modulation. A synthesis technique in which the harmonic content of a wave is changed over time by an oscillator or other envelope generator.

wave sequencing. Crossfading one wave into another by a single oscillator.

wavetable. A set of prewritten waveform parameters, stored in a computer for use in synthesis.

wavetable synthesis. Sound synthesis using a set of prewritten wavetables that are used to create new sounds.

Wd. Bl. Abbr. for wood block.

wedge. See stage monitor.

weg [Ger.]. Remove (e.g., Dampher weg, remove mute).

weighted action. An attribute on many synthesizers and electric keyboards in which weights and springs are added to the keys in order to give them the feel of an acoustic mechanical action.

Well-Tempered Clavier. Published in 1722, a book of preludes and fugues composed by J. S. Bach in all twelve keys to demonstrate the versatility of equal temperament.

West Coast jazz. A calm and laid-back style of 1950s jazz that developed in San Francisco and Los Angeles in reaction to the more frenetic East Coast bebop scene. Often thought of as a subgenre of cool jazz.

Western music. (1) Referring to the classical music tradition of Europe and North America. (2) Folk music of the West in the United States. Also known as "cowboy music."

western swing. A subgenre of country music heavily influenced by swing jazz, which utilizes strings, drums, bass, saxes, piano, and steel guitar.

wet. A signal that has a large amount of effect or processing added to it; e.g., lots of reverb.

whammy bar. A device attached to the tailpiece or bridge of an electric guitar, which enables the player to raise or lower the pitch of the strings and create vibrato and pitch bends.

whirling dervish. An energetic, spinning dance with its origins in Muslim and Sufi religious sects.

white noise. Sound created by combining all audible frequencies. See black sound.

white note. A note with an open head; e.g., a whole or half note.

whole-half scale. See octatonic scale and Scales in the Appendix.

whole note. A note held for the duration of four quarter notes, written as a stemless, unfilled, oblong shape on a space or line.

whole rest. A rest held for the duration of four quarter rests, written as a short, filled-in rectangle hanging from a line on a staff.

whole step. The interval of a major second.

whole tone. See whole step.

whole-tone scale. A six-note (hexatonic) scale in which all adjacent notes are a whole step apart. See Scales in the Appendix.

wind band. An ensemble of wind instruments.

wind chimes. A set of hanging bells or pitched rods that sound when shaken or struck by a player or when moved by the wind.

wind controller. A MIDI-based wind instrument.

wind ensemble. See concert band.

wind machine. A mechanical device that imitates the sound of wind and is used for special effects.

winds. (1) The group of woodwind instruments. (2) All wind instruments.

wolf tone. A grating tone produced by an instrument (most often string) either due to imperfections in its construction or through vibrations causing a difference tone.

wood block. See temple blocks.

woodshedding. See shed.

Woodstock. The music festival held in Woodstock, New York in 1969, that was a pivotal moment in rock history and culture of the period. Many of the top acts of the day performed there, including Jimi Hendrix, Richie Havens, Janis Joplin, Santana, Joe Cocker, the Who, and Ravi Shankar, among others.

woodwind. Blown instruments, including the flute and all reed instruments, which were originally made from wood. See also aerophone.

woofer. A loudspeaker that broadcasts low frequencies.

word clock. A synchronizing signal that uses digital data words to represent sample values.

word extension. A line that is connected to the end of a word or syllable under a series of notes in a song or vocal composition to designate that the word or vowel is to be sung as a melisma.

word painting. See text painting.

work song. A repetitive and rhythmic song accompanying repetitious work.

world beat. A broad musical genre that includes non-Western music with heavy influences of western pop and rock.

world music. A general, unspecific term usually meaning all non-Western music.

wound string. A guitar, bass, violin, or other instrument string that has a core around which a thin wire has been wrapped.

wow. In a tape-recording system, slow variations (less than 5 Hz) brought on by fluctuations in the transport system.

Wrecking Crew. A group of studio musicians who played on hundreds of popular music albums in the 1960s.

XLR connector. A professional-level balanced audio connector, typically with three pins on the male plug.

X notehead. A notehead that has an "X" replacing the usual oval to indicate that the note is to be played without a definite pitch.

Xyl. Abbr. for xylophone.

xylophone. A high-pitched percussion instrument made with wooden bars, which are laid out like a piano keyboard and are struck with mallets.

Yellow Book. A specifications document that includes error correction, track requirements, and other specifics for CD-ROMs.

yodel. A style of singing associated with the Swiss Alps in which the singer moves rapidly from normal chest voice to high falsetto.

YouTube. An online repository of video and music.

zart [Ger.]. Tenderly.

Zarzuela. A genre of Spanish opera in which spoken words are interspersed with singing.

Z-complement. In set theory, two sets sharing the same interval vector.

Zeitmass [Ger.]. Tempo.

ziemlich [Ger.]. Rather.

zill. See finger cymbals.

zimbalon. See cimbalom.

zither. A wooden stringed instrument that is plucked or strummed.

Z-related. See Z-complement.

zurna. Balkan oboe.

zusammen [Ger.]. In unison.

zydeco. A genre of music from Cajun Louisiana that is an upbeat mixture of rhythm and blues, rock, Caribbean, French, and country and western music. The accordion and fiddle often feature prominently.

APPENDICES

A. SCALES

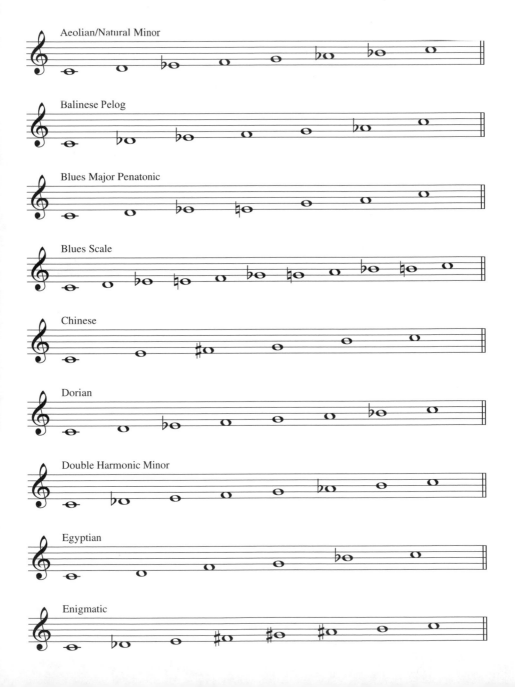

Aeolian/Natural Minor

Balinese Pelog

Blues Major Penatonic

Blues Scale

Chinese

Dorian

Double Harmonic Minor

Egyptian

Enigmatic

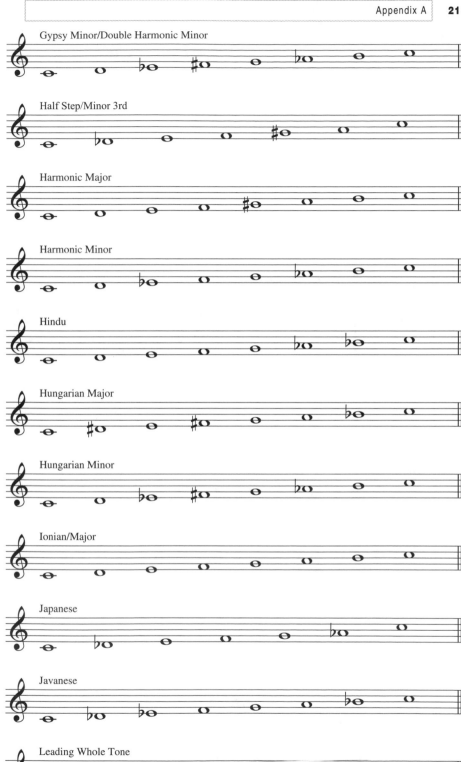

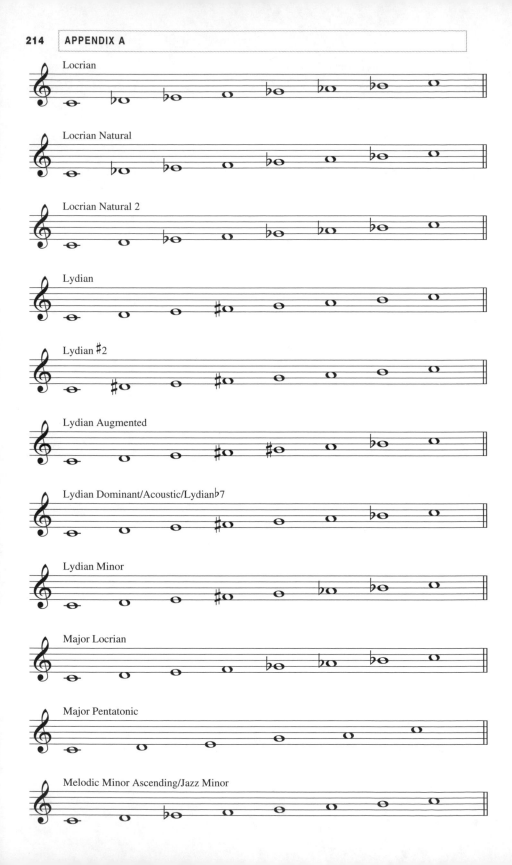

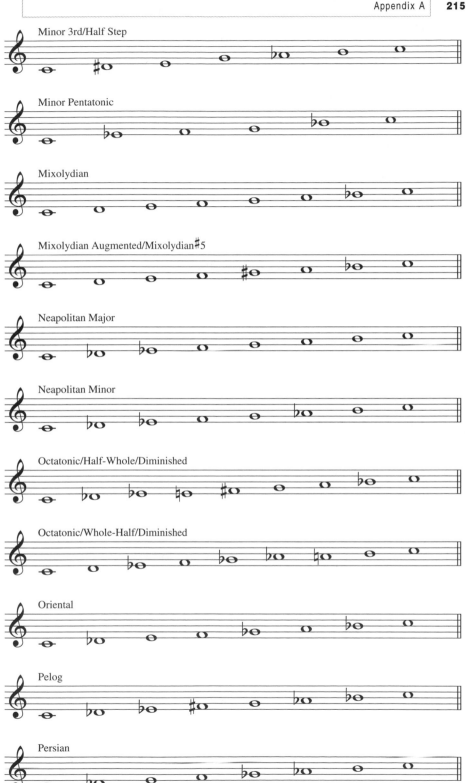

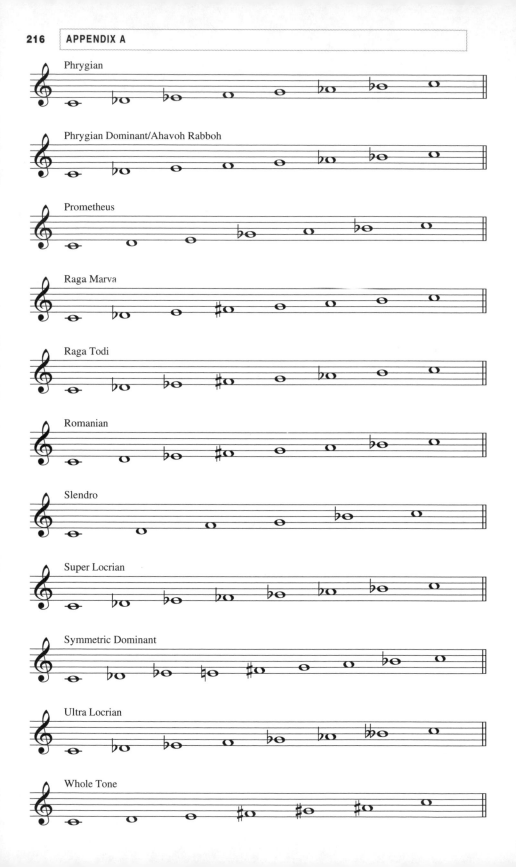

B. CHORD SYMBOL SUFFIXES

Quality	Abbreviations	Examples	Notes for C Root
major	(none), Ma, Maj, M, △	C	C E G
minor	–, mi, min, m	C– or Cmi	C E♭ G
suspended 2	sus2	Csus2	C D G
suspended 4	sus4	Csus4	C F G
diminished	dim, º	Cdim	C E♭ G♭
augmented	aug, +	Caug	C E G#
five	5	C5	C G
sixth	6	C6 C–6	C E G A C E♭ G A
seventh	7	CMaj7 C7 C7♭5 Caug7 C–7 C–(Maj7) Cdim7 Cdim(Maj7) C7sus4	C E G B C E G B♭ C E G♭ B♭ C E G♯ B♭ C E♭ G B♭ C E♭ G B C E♭ G♭ B♭♭ C E♭ G♭ B C F G B♭
half diminished	mi7♭5, –7♭5, ø	C–7♭5 or Cmi7♭5	C E♭ G♭ B♭
tensions	♭9, 9, ♯9, 11, ♯11, ♭13, 13	Note: Usage is subject to context. Not all tensions are available on all chords. C7(9, ♯11, 13)	 C E G B♭ D F♯ A

ABOUT THE AUTHOR

Photo by Tatiana Holway

Kari Henrik Juusela is a Finnish American composer, performer, and educator who presently serves as dean of the Professional Writing and Music Technology Division at Berklee College of Music in Boston, Massachusetts.

In addition to writing music in styles ranging from pop to contemporary classical, he enjoys playing and recording the cello, bass, guitar, piano, tabla, and the Finnish kantele. His compositions have won numerous awards from such organizations as the Vienna State Opera, the International Trumpet Guild, the London Chamber Music Society, the Composer's Guild, GASTA, and ASCAP. He has also won the International Red Stick Composition Competition, the San Francisco Art Song Competition, the American Songwriting Awards Contest, and the Aliénor Harpsichord Composition Contest.

His works have been performed at many important venues including Carnegie Hall and Tchaikovsky Hall by internationally acclaimed ensembles and performers, as well as by numerous rock, pop, and jazz groups.

Dr. Juusela holds degrees from the University of Maryland, Georgia State University, and Berklee College of Music. His music is published by ISG Publications, MuusJuus Music, and Yelton Rhodes Music, and recorded on ERM, Beauport Classical, Lakeside Records, Capstone Records, and MuusJuus Music.